CW01521721

FROM LEICESTERSHIRE

Edited by Emma Marsden

First published in Great Britain in 2000 by
YOUNG WRITERS
Remus House,
Coltsfoot Drive,
Woodston,
Peterborough, PE2 9JX
Telephone (01733) 890066

Copyright Contributors 2000

HB ISBN 0 75431 912 1
SB ISBN 0 75431 913 X

FOREWORD

This year, the Young Writers' Future Voices competition proudly presents a showcase of the best poetic talent from over 42,000 up-and-coming writers nationwide.

Successful in continuing our aim of promoting writing and creativity in children, our regional anthologies give a vivid insight into the thoughts, emotions and experiences of today's younger generation, displaying their inventive writing in its originality.

The thought, effort, imagination and hard work put into each poem impressed us all and again the task of editing proved challenging due to the quality of entries received, but was nevertheless enjoyable. We hope you are as pleased as we are with the final selection and that you continue to enjoy *Future Voices From Leicestershire* for many years to come.

CONTENTS

John Cleveland College

Laura Robinson	49
Crystal Simpson	50
Simon Hill	51
Claire Thomas	52
Nikole Harrison	52
Ashley Paxton	53
Sam Cuthew	53
Charlotte Silvers	54
Daniel Gunn	55
Philip Hayes	56
Michael Burton	56
Matthew Price	57
Vicki Wright	57
Clare Palmer	58
Andrew Cartledge	58
Leila Sadeghi	59
Mathew McDermott	60
Joel Harris	60
Andrea Knight	61
Katie King	62
Samantha Prosser	63
Lindsay James	64
Sarah O'Connor	65
Maria Bacon	66
Sam Byard	67
Robert Hollows	68
John Pearson	68
Dana Paton	69
Natalie Jones	69
Elizabeth Topp	70
Allison Hayton	71
Ainsley Lewinsohn	72
Michelle Boyd	72
Louiz Burrage	73
Charlotte Woodley	74

Laura Bray	74
Aden Woodhouse	75
Rachel Holt	76
Elizabeth Starbuck	76
Katy Lees	77
Lauren Martin	78
Laura Altenhofen	78
Jenna Short	79
Garry Payne	80
Michael Hemming	81
Hannah Cockburn	82
Andrew Marshall	83
Daniel Steele	84
Lisa Farrant	85
Sam Cole	86
James Wilkinson	86
Thomas Snelgrove	87
Emma Rees-Jones	88
Kathryn Everton	88
Isabel Toy	89
Keira Derbyshire	90
Gemma Shepherd	90
Jennifer Harvey	91
Richard Donnachie	91
Charlene Richardson	92
Maria Jackson	93
Gary Betts	94
Laura Davey	95
Michelle Styles	96

Loughborough High School

Krupa Trivedi	96
Imogen Mitchell	97
Sally Robinson	98
Katie Gotheridge	99
Hannah Thomas	100

William Bradford Community College

The Poems

SPRING

S   pring is here
P   eople spring-cleaning
R   oses coming out
I   n the spring newborn animals
N   ew life everywhere
G   etting near to summer.

Charles Harris (13)

IVORY PEARL

As white as an elephant's tusk,
The pearly white,
Shines in the sun.
Glistening,
Gleaming,
Against the dull grey.
As shiny as a unicorn's coat
And the curly horn,
Upon its head.
As creamy
As the spherical ball,
Found in the sea.
Shining in the sun,
Shining so bright,
The pearly colour,
Distinct,
In the light.

Lewis Jones (12)
Harry Carlton School

ANOTHER WORLD

When will the door open?
If I jump through,
Into the black midnight sky.
Flying above the world,
What will I see?
Will I look at you all and laugh
Or cry?
Floating above the world
And then back through the door
Into my bed.
Telling everyone I see about my trip
To another world
Where there was peace, harmony,
People cared about the world around them,
Everyone spoke with one voice,
In harmony.

Hannah Lacy (12)
Harry Carlton School

2000

The millennium is coming
Two thousand years ago
Parties are being planned now
Things don't move too slow

Will the computers go
Or will we all be dead?
Whatever happens on that night
We'll paint the towns red

As the world counts down the days
The hours, minutes and seconds
What will happen at twelve-o-one?
The mystery starts to beckon

The millennium is coming now
Two thousand years ago
The night will be a surprise to all
But how are we to know?

Jennifer Straw (14)
Harry Carlton School

YELLOW!

Yellow is the sun
That shines in the sky
Corn is yellow
Picked from the fields
It is also the butter
That runs through your fingers
Leaves are yellow when they
Fall in autumn
Wasps are yellow
When they come in summer
Yellow is a sunflower
A daffodil, a buttercup
That sits in the bottom of your garden
A big sour lemon
A big fat pepper is yellow
Custard with apple pie.

Sophie Blundell (12)
Harry Carlton School

A Warming Christmas Dream

It was the night before Christmas
and my head was bundled with thoughts.
I was sleeping but dreaming about everything you can imagine -
fairies, the nutcracker, lights and angels.
I didn't want the dream to stop because it made me feel
good about myself.

I felt a gush of wind hit me
and an angel brushed my face.
I could image fairies dancing upon my feet
and the Christmas spirit lingered through the air.
Christmas lights flew around,
but then made way for the nutcracker sound.

Crackers started banging and
poppers started popping.
I could feel the log fire blazing up,
filling me with warmth and security.
Presents started filling the room.
My mittens and my hat brightly glowed
and tree decorations hung off my window.

I started thinking about the meaning of Christmas
and what it meant to my family.
To my brother it meant presents and nice food.
To my mum it meant love and happiness
and to me and my dad it meant the birth of baby Jesus.

I could hear faint carol singing from the church
and could see in my mind money being donated to charity.
I felt so good inside that I wanted to be part of that charity
and do something to help one way or another.
My heart was reaching out to the lonely and hungry this Christmas
and I would pray for them and hope that maybe a Christmas miracle
would happen.

Next I thought about how lucky I was
just to have a roof over my head
and fresh, healthy food and water on my table.
Some people do not appreciate how lucky they are
and take things for granted.

Hannah Clarke (14)
Harry Carlton School

GREEN

Green as
Emeralds shining
In a rock.
As green as
A crocodile in
A murky
Muddy river.
Green equals
Goo!
Green is camouflage
Seeking in the jungle.
Green as a soldier's
Combat trousers.
As green as a plant.
Green as a horrible
Smelly swamp.
Green is tree tops
Rapidly disappearing.

Adam Torr (11)
Harry Carlton School

NEW BEGINNING

Look through the door,
What can you see?
What will it bring?

Step into happiness,
Step into freedom,
A new dawn of a new beginning.

The door of the future,
The key to the kingdom.

Step into heaven,
Far from hell,
Visit new worlds.

New places,
New boundaries to cross,
New blue clear oceans to see.

See the flowers in their radiance of colours,
All the animals united as one,
Visit a place where no hunger, no poverty exists.
Look through the door,
It holds the key to the kingdom.

Gemma Neath (12)
Harry Carlton School

FUTURE VOICES

The robots like blocks of steel,
Cold-hearted and hulking,
Marching at right angles,
Computerised to act as they do.

Eyes like zombies,
With heads which are square,
The future scares me if it's like this,
Computers killed our world.

Simon Golds (14)
Harry Carlton School

CORINTHIAN BLUE

Corinthian blue is the sight you see on a beach,
You look up,
There's the sky,
Sparkling as clouds pass by,
You see the sea,
The waves crashing,
Fizzing against steady rocks,
You see blue
In a meadow,
When tiny bluebells start to sway,
In the cold misty air
Of a summer's day,
Corinthian blue is
The sight of loneliness
Tingling all around you.
Bubbles popping
Out of a glistening glass.
Fizzing and loudly,
Awakening you,
Icicles fall onto your wind-washed face,
As coldness fills the air.

Fiona Hale (12)
Harry Carlton School

YELLOW IS . . .

Yellow is vibrant
jolly and bright.
It's also the stars
shining at night.
Yellow is lemons
and buttercups.
And the shining sun
when it comes up.
Yellow's the colour
of my pencil case.
It also beams from
a proud face.
Yellow is custard
lumpy and thick.
Yellow is speedy
rapid and quick.
Yellow is a starfish
in the sea.
Yellow is the best
colour for me.

Melissa Nevers (12)
Harry Carlton School

GREEN

Green is a grassy bit of land glowing
Green is an apple growing in a tree
Green lives out in the open
Green is a football pitch
Green is a caterpillar eating a nettle
Green is a big green carpet that goes on and on.

Michael Taylor (11)
Harry Carlton School

BLUE

Blue, as the seas great waves of water splash,
As the boy runs and jumps.
It's the lush blue waters of a swimming pool.
Makes the water more tempting.
Flows out of a pen onto a sheet of paper.
On a foggy beach
As I look out across the aqua mist.
On a rainy day
When I feel blue
I step into a puddle.
The sun in the deep blue sky
Appears to look like a sapphire.
A blueberry in my fruit bowl,
A diamond in a mine.
The colour of blue
Makes you feel good and refreshed
   Except
For a rainy day.

Joseph Booth (11)
Harry Carlton School

LIME-GREEN

Lime-green is the colour of flower stems and fresh leaves.
Lime-green is the colour of a young, clean frog.
Lime-green is the colour of fresh green grass.
Lime-green is the colour of a fat, runny felt-tip.
Lime-green is the colour of a bunch of fresh, unripe bananas.
Lime-green is the colour of a fresh, juicy kiwi.
Lime-green is the colour of a green, tender apple.

Lawrie-Louise Whitchurch (12)
Harry Carlton School

FUTURE VOICES

The poor, destitute man scurries along the beach,
Looking for anything that could provide his family with their next meal.

The rich, wealthy man relaxes on the beach,
Looking at the end of his fishing line, waiting for a bite.

The poor, destitute man finds the carcass of a crab
And slips it into his pocket.

The rich, wealthy man has a bite on the end of his line,
He reels it in and has a 10lb cod. He throws it back in.

The poor, destitute man watches in utter disgust.
The rich man laughs.

This is what is happening in the world at the moment,
Is it right that millions of people are starving all over the world?

Is it right that third world countries have to pay millions of pounds
                                        debt every day,
When thousands of people who live in those countries die every day
                                        of starvation?

Jill Campbell (14)
Harry Carlton School

ORANGE

Oranges are orange and they are very nice,
Orange is warm and brightens up the house.
Marmalade is orange, that you spread on your toast,
The sun is orange, that makes you want to roast.

Sister with her orange hair,
It makes you want to stop and stare.
Orange is a warming colour,
It makes you want to get under the covers.

Autumn is orange, with orange leaves,
In the blistering, windy breeze.
Orange is sunset, in the sky,
Now it's time to say goodbye!

Chris Wade (11)
Harry Carlton School

THE KEY TO A NEW WORLD

The door of wisdom opens and shuts,
With werewolves howling in the moonlight,
Rocky mountains with wonderful
Sights of countryside,
Wide, big rivers streaming away,
With bushbabies in the trees
And big pandas eating fresh fish.
Beautiful sights and sounds,
Echoing through the door to heaven,
Gorgeous fresh, clean oceans step into happiness,
Mountains reach the goodness of the volcano,
Look down and see sunny bubbling views,
The land of God's with new creatures
Born every minute
And very sadly things dying
But that still does not beat
The echoing view down.
Go, go, further into heaven
And sing, show me heaven, show me love
And then . . .
Birds parrots, insects and mammals with every creature,
In the hearted living world!

Dan Adams (12)
Harry Carlton School

COOL JADE

Cool jade dancing in the wind
Gleaming in the water
Sizzling on a warm summer's day
Cool jade, rising into the atmosphere
And beyond
Cool jade like stars flying by
Waterfalls crashing into the rocks
Like paints in a pot
Cool jade like a refreshing
Handful of water from a spring
Cool jade, the refreshing sight
Cool jade, the colour of a rainbow
Like the blue planet Pluto
Cool jade, the colour of the sea
And the refreshing drink of blueberry
Cool jade like the bottom of the ocean
Cool jade swimming with the fishes
Cool jade, leaving without a trace.

Scott Kent (12)
Harry Carlton School

MILLENNIUM!

The new Millennium's drawing near.
I have new hope for this brand new year,
No crime, no drugs, no poverty or war,
To be healthy and wealthy,
Not sad or poor.

People living in harmony,
Together all as one,
No fighting other people,
May all the wars be done.

Here's hoping for a future
That's good for everyone,
With peace the whole world over
When we reach the Millennium.

Katherine Bott (14)
Harry Carlton School

CALYPSO (GREEN)

Calypso is leaves,
Hanging on tall trees,
Tropical rainforests,
An enemy, weeds.
Slime on stones,
A young mermaid's tail,
A calm clear sea,
On which a boat will sail.
A baby's eyes,
Huge slimy frogs,
Flying green flies,
Soft, damp moss.
Calypso is salad,
An empty field,
Uncut grass,
Patterns on a shield.
Proud, blooming flowers,
Shiny, small emeralds,
The sight of fresh mint,
Another enemy, mould!

Louise Ungless (12)
Harry Carlton School

THE STARS

Stars go a-twinkling
a handful a-sprinkling
shining so brightly
some only slightly
A bright star sign
the Orion's belt line
A black night sky
above me so high
I see the crescent moon
could be full soon
A bewitching place
seeing those stars made of lace
Seven hours later I shall see
the dawn musk ahead of me
then goodbye to the stars.

Rebecca Clay (14)
Harry Carlton School

BLUE

Blue is the colour of the sky,
The colour of cold snow and ice.
A colour of a swimming pool,
Feel the cold of the air; cool!
Ink and clothes and paper too,
When you are sad, you feel blue!

Blue is the colour of wallpaper and paint!
The colour of a sad saint.
A big and shiny brand new car,
As I wish upon my lucky star.
Furniture, chairs and tables,
The colour of a brand new stable.

Blue is my favourite colour,
Well after all, it is a stunner!
Now it's time for me to go,
For me to paint my toe! (Nail)

Charlotte Thomson-Bialy (11)
Harry Carlton School

LADYBIRD

The ladybird opens her beautiful wings to the cloudy sky,
A flash of lightning is clearly seen
By her widening eye.
She gives a dainty leap into the cold and stormy air
And struggles frantically,
Then her wings begin to tear.
The rain beats hard upon her,
Like a savage to the drum.
She's falling very quickly,
Now her time is almost done.
She bounces off a leaf
And floats down onto the ground,
She's like a tiny bubble, very small and almost round.
Finally, she lands
Like a feather small and light.
She's trying to recover
From her badly bruising plight.
At last she surrenders
And her spirit cries out
'Is this all there is to life, just for nought?'

Eleanor Mckinley (14)
Harry Carlton School

KINGFISHER BLUE

Is the colour of kingfishers,
Diving in ice-cold water
And shimmering shells,
On the bottom of the clear blue sea,
Sapphires shining,
In with the forget-me-nots,
The clear blue sky on a
Cold winter's night,
Blueberries drawn in ink
And dolphins jumping,
Fireworks on the millennium,
Porpoises playing in the harbour,
Bluebells carpet the forest floor,
A whale alone in the water,
The shipwreck lying alone,
On the sea bed,
The polar bear in the ice-cold
And its cubs playing by themselves.

Hannah Owen (12)
Harry Carlton School

ICE-CREAM YELLOW

Swirling cream
The taste is supreme
I love ice-cream
It fills me up and cheers me up
You can stock it up
And put a cherry on the top
And then when you have done all that
Sit back and sleep.

Chris Michaelides (12)
Harry Carlton School

THE DOOR OF A NEW WORLD

The new world,
Will have no poverty.

Life opens the door
And out there,
There is a new world.
There is a key,
To your life.
With friends, glory, nature, rivers and oceans.
Flowers will change colour in the new world.
Lonely people walking down the
Never-ending streets hand in hand.
The fields lead to nowhere.
The angels singing hear the
Echoing in the lonely streets.
There are mountains to climb,
Boundaries to cross.
Hear the voice of God,
Speaking to lonely people.

Stacey Hunt (12)
Harry Carlton School

A DOOR TO A NEW BEGINNING

What would it be like, maybe flying cars, or carpets too?
Would people's houses still be on the ground or hover in the air?
Would trees be a mile high, and plants be two meters tall?
Would tigers be extinct, would bugs rule the world?
Would dinosaurs be extinct or very alive and eat everything in sight?
Would pollution be no more?
Would people talk to animals and animals shout back?
I wonder what a new beginning would be like, I wonder . . .

Michael Cole (12)
Harry Carlton School

HELL

This place as hot as the sun,
where all evil is set loose.
Satan sitting there on his throne,
rows of tortured souls begging for *mercy!*

Satan's workers,
as black as evil itself,
torturing the souls of the bad,
snapping the backs of the evil,
destroying all faith in the good.

All of Satan's workers,
destroying all who are evil,
as the souls of the good,
look down from heaven,
and shiver with fear.

Andrew Robinson (14)
Harry Carlton School

LOVE OR HATE?

Love or hate is a difficult question.
How do you know when you hate someone?
How do you know when you don't?

Love is when people make you happy.
Having someone to love you is what makes you want to live.
When they are kind, friendly and generous
Makes you warm inside.

When they are mean to you,
Offensive, horrible and brutal,
Makes you cold and unhappy inside
Like you are alone, no one to care for you at all.

Loving someone makes you happy.
To know that they are happy because you made them
Happy is what it is all about.

Hating someone makes you sad, knowing that they are
Upset because you made them upset.

Love or hate is a difficult question.
How do you know when you love someone?
How do you know when you don't?

Louise Smalley (14)
Harry Carlton School

CATISFACTION!

Sitting tall and proud,
With her furry black ears acting as a crown,
Her lovely green eyes twinkle merrily
And her black beard bobs happily.
Her little white socks curl up and under,
As she lays her body very sweetly,
One black and white paw,
Stretched over a cuddly toy.

She leans forward,
Stretching her neck,
Daintily sniffing the toy spider's red legs.
Licking her chops,
She looks around,
Then lowers her head
And crossly she miaows!

Fiona Cooper (15)
Harry Carlton School

MY FUTURE

Down into the deep, dark mind,
Where all is new,
Stands my future.
I walk to my future and see Heaven,
Angels flying all around me,
All I hear is humming.
Angels fly in the shape of an Earth,
Angels have colourful wings,
If only I could fly.
What would life be
Without angels?
They give me the key to my wisdom,
I lie in bed thinking,
What could I do with my future?
What could I do with it?

Nikita Goodman (12)
Harry Carlton School

YELLOW

The shining sun shimmers in the sky
Lumpy custard sitting on a pie
Daffodils flowering in the spring
Melon succulent, fit for a king
Golden hair shining bright
Yellow curtains keeping out the winter night
Sparkling paint glistening on the door
Soft bananas melting on your toast
Yolk of an egg dripping down the shell.

Grace Smart (11)
Harry Carlton School

BLACK?

They say that green is the new black,
But I don't really understand it
Because last year they said that red was the new black.
So what is the colour I'm seeing?
They told me at school that black isn't a colour,
So if all the colours are a new black,
That means black is every colour.
So what is black?
In English we were told about this so-called black,
It's supposed to be dark and sinister,
A colour to be mourned.
Rainbows are black,
Clothes are black,
The world is black,
We are black.

Rosalind Winton (14)
Harry Carlton School

THE COLOUR OF GOLD

Gold is the colour of syrup that glistens on the surface
                of your porridge in the morning.
Gold is the colour of straw on a farm on a frosty morning.
Gold is the colour of a lion's fur in the long straw.
Gold is the colour of honey resting in a jar.
Gold is the colour of a ring upon your hand or the sand
                on a hot and sunny day.

Gold is a happy colour that brings happiness into the heart!

Tom Sellers (12)
Harry Carlton School

PURPLE

Purple is the colour of the flowers
And the groovy colours of Austin Powers,
Felt tips, pencils, crayons and a girl's bedroom,
Purple shines throughout the world.
In the summer I have my purple sunglasses
And the cool juice of Ribena.
In the winter I have my scarf.
Purple makes me cheerful when I'm down in the dumps
And it's the colour of marshmallow 'flumps'.
On my purple bike or on my cousin's trike
You can splash through the puddles.
Purple makes you dizzy and silly
And sometimes is the colour of my friend Tilly.
Purple is the new millennium,
Purple is the generation,
Purple never fades.

Megan Wheatcroft (11)
Harry Carlton School

BLUE, BLUE, BLUE COLOUR

Blue is the colour of a blue poem containing blue ink.
The blue sea carries the blue whales and dolphins.
Blue is the colour of fireworks sailing up into the dark night sky.
Blue are the feelings, a lonely blue bird in the morning.
Blue is the fresh air in early winter dawn.
A girl wearing a blue bobble hat blows her blue bubblegum.
A blue spotted dragon feels cold.
An electric eel swims with fish.
Blue hundreds and thousands sit upon the cake.

Mandy Barnard (12)
Harry Carlton School

YELLOW

Yellow is a melon
As bright as the sun.
And yellow is the corn in the field
And yellow is a bright bird
In the sky.
People in yellow trousers
Running here and there.
Teachers with bright yellow
Folders as bright as a daffodil
And a banana.
The sweet smelling scent
Of a daffodil gleaming in the sun.
People running in bright yellow
Hats running to and fro.
I love yellow, it's my favourite colour.

Lauren Severn (12)
Harry Carlton School

OUR FUTURE ENVIRONMENT

The world has become a shameful place
Piles of litter are seen everywhere and in every space
Parks are now a bed of litter, and every day getting thicker
In the countryside no children play, towns and cities are an
                                            industrialised bay
Cities are full of factories with machines
Everyone is lazy, but this is not a dream
This display is our future
Our future children's home and these are their future voices,
                                      which are future groans.

Joseph Winton (14)
Harry Carlton School

SPACE

The roar of the engines starts
Everyone looks on anxiously
The rocket begins to rise
Gently ascending in a gravity-defying splendour.

The noise fades away
And everyone is still
Only now does the thought touch them
And the silence is shattered.

People begin bustling about
Congratulating each other heartily
For the realisation has dawned on them
That this is the start of a new era.

The rocket is carrying people's hopes into space
Hoping for success
For the rocket is the first piece of a station
A new home in space.

The station will provide home to many
Hundreds who have left Earth
Searching for a new life
And a new challenge to conquer.

Hopefully the station will be there in the future
A home away from home
For weary travellers and crew
Continuing the journey of discovery.

Peter Kay (15)
Harry Carlton School

ELECTRIC BLUE

An exciting colour,
  bursting with freshness,
An exploding firework,
Deep with sensation,
A warm breeze on a cool summer's morn,
Bubblegum and blueberries,
  a new chemical is formed,
Frozen icicles
And whispering waves,
Rippling shores in
Eerie dark caves,
Blue tits and kingfishers,
Fresh fish and blue whales,
Bluebells and lavender,
On a dull frosty morn,
Catching the sunlight,
Blinding us all,
Blue is cold,
Blue is warm,
Depending on whether your mood is forlorn,
A cluster of shining sapphires on
  a rich lady's hand,
A puddle of sea water,
  on white tropical sand,
Blue is fierce,
Blue is kind,
Depending on what's buzzing around in your mind.

Sophie Baker (12)
Harry Carlton School

COOL WATER

It's frozen water on a cold winter's day,
A clear blue sky in the summer,
It's relaxing, confusing
And a salty green sea,
It's grey-blue dolphins that swim
In the ocean,
It likes to brew a green-blue potion,
A chilling refreshment,
On a sunny summer's day,
It's the colour of rain,
That falls from the sky,
A blueberry pie,
A blue ink pen that's spilt on the floor,
It's a blue eye,
Very determined,
To do what's right.

Andrew McKibbin (12)
Harry Carlton School

FLAME RED

The red in a flame.
The colour of my pencil.
Flame red, the colour on a magazine.
The colour of blood.
Strawberries are red
And roses too.
The colour of the lid
On my mum's tin.
The colour of the tip
Of my pen.
The colour of my brother's torch.

David Arthur (11)
Harry Carlton School

ICE-CREAM 70P

It's a pale yellow,
Eat a marshmallow,
It tastes so sweet and sugary,
The colour of juicy pasta,
Looks so calm and cold,
Tastes so exciting,
Colour of fluffy wool,
Lots of different, interesting flavours,
Have an ice-cream, 70p,
It will give you lots of glee,
I love to stack it with chocolate drops,
My favourite flavour is coffee with toffee sauce,
What's your favourite flavour?
I love ice-cream, the food supreme,
Eat a lot of it.

Nick Pleasant (12)
Harry Carlton School

BLUE

Blue is the colour of the sky
Where small bluetits can fly
Blue is the colour of the wavy sea
Where big white doves come to get a drink
Raindrops are the colour of the sea
As they come splish, splash on your face
Bluebells are the shape of a ball
Which beautifully bloom in the summer and nicely smell
Blue is the colour of ink
Just like my blue pen which goes clink
Midnight blue is the colour of the purply sky
When the stars really gloom and the moon starts to go down.

Zarqa Ahmed (11)
Harry Carlton School

PEACE OR WAR?

Peace or war, is a difficult question.
Do we want to live in harmony,
Or choose to hate?
As I look into the future,
I face two doors in front of me,
One labelled with 'war' and the other with 'peace'.
I ponder about which one to choose.
Do I take the 'war' and make my life miserable,
Or do I choose 'peace' and live my life in harmony?
I split into two, wondering which one to take,
Then my mind tells me what to do.
I look around and beside my head
Are a devil and an angel telling me what to do.
The devil leads me to the door labelled 'war'
And as I walk through the door
It's hot and all I can hear is screaming and shouting and hurtful noises.
I excoriate the door and leave that world behind me,
I don't want a world with violence.
The angel leads me to the other door.
I push the door ajar,
I feel the breeze, the fresh breeze in my hair,
Flowers swaying happily in the breeze,
Everyone laughing happily in the summer sun.
I see that's the life for me
But something is holding me back, back in the past
Which I can't leave behind.
Help me choose, please help me choose
And choose the world you want too.

Helen Spencer (14)
Harry Carlton School

THE ECLIPSE

Thrusting upwards towards the sky.
The hill has risen,
The work of giants in ages gone by.

From its summit my eyes can see
The archipelago of islands
Once all one, now separated by a rising sea.

Far away in a lonely place
I see a ship
Methodically working, oblivious of my attention.

It's August the 11th
The air still with suspense
I wait with expectation.

My world darkens
I feel ever more enchanted
A chill settles.

From across the vast ocean
A shadow rushes
Engulfing my ship.

Its silent stealth
Takes a world by surprise
Time hangs suspended.

Suddenly the shadow repents
It's all over
Life carries on.

Chris Cleaver (14)
Harry Carlton School

PHOENIX YELLOW

Yellow is
The sun in the early morning light,
Bread fresh from the oven,
Bananas laying in the bowl,
Feathers of a proud golden eagle,
Dandelions swaying in the field,
Glow of a dim candlelight,
Bright skin of a tangy lemon,
Sharp beak of a sly blackbird,
Golden sand of the tropical beach,
Rich colour of a brave lion's mane,
Crispy crunch of a crunchy biscuit,
The colour of corn in the field,
Fierce roar of the fire so hot.

Craig Wood (12)
Harry Carlton School

GREEN

Green is a blade of grass,
It's a leaf on a tree,
It's a grape,
An emerald shining in the night,
A dinosaur roaring,
A crocodile standing its ground.
Green is the Exorcist that's been sick,
It's a folder full of work,
A pencil case,
It's a plate of broccoli,
Peas and spinach.
Green is an apple shining in a fruit bowl,
A pear with so much juice.

Ryan Robinson (11)
Harry Carlton School

EARTH OF THE FUTURE

The Earth will tremor with power,
Power of the people,
So much power, gloom, doom,
Too much power to handle.
The fearless people shredding the land,
To destruction and terror,
The helpless Earth abandoned,
Shipwrecked, marooned in space,
Waiting for new life, new worlds, new beginnings,
Vision of a new dawn,
A key to a kingdom,
A door to the future,
Life to land,
The oceans roar again.

Mark Allard (12)
Harry Carlton School

SIESTA SUN

Yellow is the colour of fireworks popping and
Sparklers sparkling on a bonfire night.
A star glittering silently in the dusky night-time sky.
A daffodil and daisy in the summer breeze.
A warm and cheerful colour yellow is.
A yellow frog on a lily pad
As buzzing bees buzz in the summer meadow,
As a duck quacks and a canary sings adventurously.
The sun roars to be set free.
A colourful colour yellow is.
As a yellow dinghy set off on a sunset day,
As honey was spread on a yellow sponge cake,
Yellow is bright as you can see.

Anna Shahatit (12)
Harry Carlton School

LIVE OR DIE?

Live or die? It's a difficult question,
People often wonder in mystery.
Live long? Die young? Leave your life behind
And be a part of history.
But if nobody knows,
(When you're all alone)
That you're gone
And as bitter as a stone.
Live or die? It's a difficult question
And it is all left up to fate.

Live and be merry,
Enjoy all of what life can bring.
Love all the people around you,
Feel as noble as a king.
But when it comes down to it, is this how you feel
About your life,
About your world,
With all of its worries and all of its strife?

Live or die? Die or live?
The choice, not up to you,
To live and be sad, to die and be forgotten,
But what do you want to do?
Be killed?

Nicola Bilton (14)
Harry Carlton School

WHAT IS BLUE?

Blue is the sea when it crashes on the rocks,
Blue is the colour of my warm winter sock.

Blue is the colour of my blue ink,
Blue is the colour of the kitchen sink.

Blue is the colour of my little lamp
But I can't use it when I'm at camp.

Blue is the colour of my bedroom wall
When I'm dancing at some balls.

Blue is the colour of my lovely blue eyes
And my mum knows when I'm telling lies.

Blue is the colour of the blue, blue sky,
When the birds fly so, so high.

Blue is the colour of the swimming pool
When I jump in it I feel cool.

Blue is the colour of my T-shirt
And all the boys come and flirt.

Blue is the name of my favourite song
And I feel blue when I go wrong.

Blue makes me big when I feel small
Blue is the bestest colour of all.

Amy Bell (12)
Harry Carlton School

NEVER KNOWING!

Waiting down the front line,
my gun held high above my head,
never knowing, never knowing,
when the first gunshots
are going to go up to the sky,
when I am going to fall
to the ground ready for the next shot.
Crawling along the floor in the mud,
my face splattered
with mud, water and left over food,
never knowing, never knowing,
when it's my turn
to meet the others up in heaven.
The first shot flying,
whipping across the sky.
It's my turn to go,
farewell!
Never knowing, never knowing.

Rebecca Lovatt (14)
Harry Carlton School

FUTURE VOICES

Voices are in my head
What shall I do as a job?
What college would I go to?
The future is a strange thing
We never know what is in front of us
But we know what is behind us
A new future is made every minute
One ends every minute
The future can be boring
The future can be great
The future can be exciting
The future can be strange
What does the future hold?
We hope life may be good
Will my life be fulfilling?
The future is right in front of us
But we can't see it.

Chris Wakefield (12)
Harry Carlton School

Nobody Knows

A door,
A door to freedom,
A door to fantasy,
A door to a better world,
Nobody knows.
What will the future bring?
Hope and mercy to people who have none,
A lost world that nobody knows,
A strange place bewildered in time.
A maze of flowers, fantasy and radiance,
A glistening lake and mountains to climb,
A world of blue skies, wind and sun,
A fresh new look for the scenery around us,
A strange place bursting with magic,
A spirit of goodness,
No war,
No poverty,
United with your soul.
A door,
A door to freedom,
A door to fantasy,
A door to a better world,
Nobody knows.

Lucy Moores (13)
Harry Carlton School

HUMMINGBIRD YELLOW

Hummingbird, the colour of cheese,
So bold and bright,
A light warm breeze.
Buzzing bees,
On a fresh morning,
The sun through the trees,
Children are yawning.
Ripe bananas,
Lovely and sweet,
Mouth-watering lemons,
What a treat.
Vibrant glimmering
Tropical birds,
Soft and fluffy,
Lemon curds.
Roses so sweet,
Yellow and bright,
Grow in the garden,
What a great sight.
The sunflowers grow
Oh so high,
One foot higher
They will reach the sky.

Hannah Chaplin (12)
Harry Carlton School

GREEN

Green is the grass
In the fields so fair.
Green is the fresh smell in the air.
Rolling hills and sloping valleys,
It's a colour that makes you dilly and dally.
This pen in my hand is also green.
Grapes, melons, apples, unripe bananas.
Feeling ill, wearing pyjamas,
Socks, T-shirts, jumpers and coats.
Wrapping paper could be green.
Christmas tree and their decorations.
Green is a lime,
My room's lime green.
Nail varnish could be green,
But you wold look a bit strange.
Aliens are the colour green,
So is the thread my mother is sewing with.
The Macmillan charity box is too.
Green is a very popular colour.

Hope Dawkins (11)
Harry Carlton School

NEW WORLD!

I had a dream, a dream of the future.
With open doors and no hunger,
Blue skies, oceans.
It will be like you have stepped into
A world full of happiness.
This world is full of hope, glory,
Beauty and goodness.
The people of this new world have
Mountains to climb,
Bridges to cross,
Then they go up the stairs to heaven or
Down the stairs to hell.
They can go to the kingdom of wisdom
So they become
Spirits of goodness or
Angels of mercy.
Rainbow shooting across the sky.
Explosion of colour makes
The whole new world colourful.
This is the new millennium.

Jenny Bott (12)
Harry Carlton School

YOU REACH THAT SPECIAL DOOR

An open door,
Stepping from one place to the next,
Will it be nowhere?
Or,
Will it be somewhere
Where nobody has ever been before?
Is it a fantasy
Where all is good and pure?
Or is it a hallowed undiscovered place?
It might be a place at peace
'Heaven', yes it might be.
But what if it's not?
What if it is the undiscovered place?
Solitary,
Nowhere to go,
Nowhere to run or hide,
But then,
Maybe it's a door to somewhere,
An open door.
You'll never know until one day
You reach that special door.

Hollie Ward (12)
Harry Carlton School

A NEW DAY, A NEW TIME, A NEW WORLD

A boundary to cross
Stepping from one life to another
A peaceful life
The beginning
A new world that needs to be explored
Unknown to everyone
No hunger, no war, no poverty to harm anyone
One voice, singing to come
Unlock the door to a magical kingdom
Goodness and happiness
Hope and purity
Seeing heaven in all its glory
Freedom of all evil
A world
Shining in a radiant glow
The light from the Earth sparkles
A reflection shimmers on the ocean
Mountains to climb to reach our goals
A new day
A new time
A new world.

Sam Stevenson (12)
Harry Carlton School

OPEN THE DOOR

The door to a new world
Future, freedom
The millennium
A new era
Hopefully no more poverty
A world of happiness
A peaceful time
Blue skies
Clear oceans
Spirit of goodness
No more hunger
Look after the countryside
Let the rivers meander
Snow-topped mountains
Beautiful colours that echo
Freedom and peace
Open the door to a new world
A happy, kind new world.

Jo Horner (12)
Harry Carlton School

THE END OF THE WORLD

The end of the world
Should never come,
But what if it does?
A bomb, or a generation of wars.
Scary, if it does.
That abandoned world,
Floating in lifeless space,
Watching the Earth die.
One day,
One day it will come,
The end of our sacred, damaged Earth.
Floating away,
To doom, burn up and die.
Life will die.
Animals too.
We will have to leave,
Find a new world,
To burn up and kill.

Jonathan Hellier (12)
Harry Carlton School

THE MILLENNIUM

The dawn to a new era,
We can start fresh,
Forget all of our mistakes,
Make Third World poverty no more.
End war and fighting,
Let hell ice over and forget about it,
Stop pollution and litter.
Let it be a great world of happiness,
Hope for no racism,
No bullying or fighting,
No crime and murders.
Let there be green fields and fresh grass,
Let it be a world of peace at harmony.
Recycle and be hygenic.
Let vandalism be a thing of the past.
Make car fumes smell sweet.
Let there be a simple cure for cancer.
No leprosy or disability,
Be no poor souls,
Be no homeless people.

Adam Pearson (13)
Harry Carlton School

THE DOOR OF HOPE

Reminds me of life,
An open door,
A key to life,
It reminds me of hope,
Purity,
Glory and peace,
An honourable place, happiness,
No hunger, no poverty,
The sweet singing in the moors
And mountains, skies as blue
As the deep sea,
Mountains to climb,
To reach the glory of God,
But never quite touching,
Its curing hand,
So many things to do,
So much to see,
Boundaries to cross,
Places to go,
The door to the future.

Kayleigh Hunt (12)
Harry Carlton School

TUDOR ROSE

Red is the dust of a brick
With the red of a robin
And a bright cherry mix
With the red of a sunset
And the mellow of a lipstick
A red cape, a rose
A meadow of who knows
Poppies, mysterious love
But then, there's people
Screaming for love
Or for fire, lava and flame
Envy of war
A signal, a soar
Of anger to blood
And unhappiness
But then there's hope
A tinted light
A very, very beautiful sight
To give people a flag
Of peace
Hail! The Tudor rose.

Michelle Greaves (12)
Harry Carlton School

VICARAGE GREEN

Vicarage green is an exciting colour
Full of flavour
And full of life.
Grapes are bursting with juice.
The leaves on a flower
Swaying in the wind,
It gives the apples power
And keeps the countryside fresh.
Vicarage green is
Peas in a pod
Going pop, pop, pop
And pears drop, drop, drop.
The hedges gleam with green
And on the ground the weeds
Spread through.
Green is fresh salad
On an olive plate
And the lime green meadows
Growing sweet and tall.
It reminds me of a warm woollen jumper
On a cold winter's night.
So really, what is green?

Zoe Zurawlin (12)
Harry Carlton School

SPLASH BLUE

It's the ocean waves,
Sky on a summer's day,
Droplets of rain falling from the sky,
Splash blue is whispy clouds on a summer's day,
Morning sun on bluebells,
Tiny icicles,
It's loneliness and fear,
It's when your ears are finely tuned
And you hear the patter of tiny mice feet,
Splash blue is the sight of fish,
Swimming in shoals,
In a warm coral reef,
It's bubble in a glass,
Fizzing,
Popping,
Jumping around,
Splash blue is the dolphins,
Diving,
Splashing,
Jumping through the air,
Splash blue is the sound,
Feeling,
Loneliness,
Of an empty corridor.

Beth Hind (12)
Harry Carlton School

YELLOW

Yellow is the sun shining bright
And the moon keeping it light
Yellow is butter
That melts in your mouth
Yellow is a sunflower
Yellow is power
Yellow is the brightest
It is the lightest
Colour of all
It is the spots of Mr Blobby
It is not for people snobby
Yellow is the thing that decorates the sky
Yellow is a melon
Juicy like a lemon
Yellow is a person bubbly
Happy and fun
Yellow brings joy to everyone.

Becci Cooper (11)
Harry Carlton School

SENSES

The eyes bore deep,
Deep down, through to my soul,
Haunting me with their bright light.
I feel scared, but calm.
They look right through me,
Bewitching me.

Laura Robinson (17)
John Cleveland College

DAD

Ding,
The faint sound of a tolling bell can be heard,
Distant but still there, like a faded memory.
So long ago yet still so recent.
The heartache long and unforgiving,
Which are the past; the present; the future?
All blended into one, never moving one way or the other.
They are the same,
Something valuable and unforgettable is missing from all three;
Dad.

I look back on the many happy times we shared,
Hours filled with laughter and hours filled with silence,
For though silence was present we still knew what the other
Was thinking.
For we were and are the same.
As I am your own flesh and blood.
I am you.

They say absence makes the heart grow fonder,
You don't know how true that is,
For I know that only a miracle would put you back in my life,
You were and still partly are my world.
Parting was not our own choosing,
Although I know it was for the best.
I can never change the way I feel about you,
Dad: I love you.

Crystal Simpson (14)
John Cleveland College

A BET BETWEEN FRIENDS

I look at my watch and stick up my thumb.
The lads are all laughing. The time has come,
(It's now or never; I won't back down).
To win this bet and wear the crown.

I begin to undress, catching a young woman's eye,
(A mixed bunch of feelings, should I laugh or cry?)
But I break the gaze and continue to strip
And vow to complete my naked trip.

Slowly I rise from the cold plastic seat.
All the spectators are in for a treat.
Nobody notices; they continue to play,
But I jump over the boarding and sprint away.

Arms and legs thrashing. People just stare
But I'm running my fastest 'cause I'm totally bare,
I feel a bit foolish but my fun never ends,
All in the name of a bet between friends.

The players are smiling at my piece of fun
But the stewards are coming and I'm nearly done.
I dance with the ref to a celebratory cheer.
I know it's all over as footsteps draw near.

So now I sit naked with nothing to say,
No reason why on this cold Saturday.
I have won the bet and the money is mine.
Will it cover the cost of my definite fine?

Simon Hill (17)
John Cleveland College

LOST IN THE DEPTHS OF MY HEART

If we had forever
Then our love would never end.
I would still receive all the things
In which you used to send.
I'll never forget our first meeting
And the way you looked at me.
Our eyes were locked, my heart beat quickened
As if we were meant to be.
Your face was like the sunshine,
As if you could do no wrong.
Like when you serenade me,
With our special and favourite song.
But now you've gone and left me
To fend for myself in the world,
I miss the way you made me feel
And the way my heart would swirl.
I know that you still love me
And that we will never part
And now that you've gone and left me,
You're lost in the depths of my heart.

Claire Thomas (15)
John Cleveland College

FROG

Green and slimy and good to eat,
The best bits of a frog are its legs and feet,
A taste similar to chicken,
But I can't agree,
That frogs' legs will ever stay down inside me.

Nikole Harrison (18)
John Cleveland College

METAPHOR POEM

I am dance music,
I'm always having a good time.

I am max power,
Because I'm to the max.

I am the spring,
Because I'm always energetic.

I am the storms,
I have a short temper.

I am a bulldog,
Because I'm British.

I am judo,
Because I like having fights.

Ashley Paxton (14)
John Cleveland College

THE ONCE BRAT

Every child's a little brat,
A good one's just well trained,
So from that day and after that,
The little brat has changed.

'Please and thank you' the once brat says,
Not 'I want, gimme, now,'
And now you know the training pays,
The once brat, an angel.

Sam Cuthew (14)
John Cleveland College

LIFE

I sit here and watch nature
Surrounding me, all
So very unique but
All so identical too.
Birds' harmonious voices whistle on
The breeze - indescribable, unrecognisable -
An alien sound to my
Inner thoughts.
And every living moment filled with
The life cycle; round and
Round in a circle go God's
Inexplicable resources.
Small, powerful monsters, what purpose
Could they possibly serve? Yet their
Blood is as red and as rich as our
Own, and their minds?
We are superior yet we are microscopic
In the sphere of creation and in the
Universe; we are atoms in
Our house of good, and evil.
The forces can overpower us but so too
Can our greed and
Nourishment of
Wisdom.
Could His creations be so very
Unlike?

Charlotte Silvers (17)
John Cleveland College

MY POEM

I'm a fox,
I am cunning and sly.
I'm always on the prowl.

I am an oak,
For I am big and tall
And my roots are big.

I am a racing car,
I am fast, strong
And always take up space.

I am blue,
Because I support Chelsea
And blue is cold
Like the wind.

I am summer,
For I am warm-hearted
And I'm always liked by people.

I am chocolate,
I am sweet and tasty.

I am a diamond,
I'm expensive and I always sparkle

I am roses,
Romantic and beautiful.

Daniel Gunn (14)
John Cleveland College

METAPHOR POEM

I am a fox,
I am very sly.

I am a mini,
Slow and cute.

I am the summertime,
Bright and always happy.

I am the CN tower,
I tower above the rest.

I am a curry,
Hot and spicy.

I am orange,
Bright and happy.

Philip Hayes (14)
John Cleveland College

THE WOLF

The supernatural light of the moon shines upon you.
Your majestic presence fills me with awe.
You raise your head
And fill the air with your haunting cry.
Your strength, skill and intelligence
Amaze me.
I can only wonder why
A creature of such beauty
Can be seen as such a monster.
To me you're a creature of mystery,
A misunderstood creature of the wild.

Michael Burton (17)
John Cleveland College

FLY AWAY

Times when we are oceans apart
Your voice calls softly through the night.
And many months while you're away
The days seem so long and grey.
Time to spread our wings and fly.

Sailing 'cross the ocean spray
Gliding through the twilight mist
Drawing closer to you once again.
Past the lapping waves, beyond the fiery storms,
I see your homeland before me.
Our dreams have come true.

Standing by the chalk cliffs base,
Footsteps quicken - we're here face to face.
Now you're in my arms I'll never let you go.
It's time to spread our wings and fly.

Matthew Price (14)
John Cleveland College

HOMELESSNESS

Feeling cold and empty inside
The love you had has burned out and died.
Sometimes it's hard to understand,
When at your time of trouble and despair
No one's prepared to give you a hand.
People walk on by without a glance,
Thinking it's your fault you're stuck in this trance.
The wind whistles on and still no one cares,
Each day a thousand more stares.

Vicki Wright (17)
John Cleveland College

METAPHOR POEM!

I am a dog,
When taught properly I learn fast.

I am the colour orange,
I am very bright and colourful.

I am a pansy,
Small but beautiful.

I am a house,
Not very smart but necessary.

I am a glass of beer,
You may become addicted to me.
(Meaholic, alcoholic).

I am the Great Wall of China,
When you start at the beginning
It never ends.

Clare Palmer (14)
John Cleveland College

IF ONLY I COULD RHYME

I would like to write a poem
That would stand the test of time.
But the main large jolt to bring me to a halt
Is that I simply can't think of a rhyme.

I could write a ditty on anything,
A person, event or game;
I would not mind if I could just find,
Any two words which sound the same.

I wouldn't mind if it were long or short,
One verse would do just fine,
But I really can't see this occurring with me,
As I simply can't think of a rhyme.

Andrew Cartledge (16)
John Cleveland College

I AM

I am a hyena
Always in stitches.

I am a safe
Keeping your deepest secrets.

I am the colour red,
Loud and always noticed.

I am a sunflower
Tall and cheerful.

I am a diamond
Priceless and glowing.

I am sunshine
Vibrant and bright.

I am a palm tree
Tall and exotic.

Leila Sadeghi (14)
John Cleveland College

METAPHOR

I am the sun,
I'm always around somewhere, sometime.

I am England,
I am tactical, skilful and I never quit.

I am a mole,
I lie low and am shy around other things.

I am an armchair,
For I am laid back and comfortable.

I am silk,
I'm smooth, soft and delicate.

I am dance music,
I'm energetic
And I've got a repeated beat.

Mathew McDermott (14)
John Cleveland College

MORTIFIED

His face felt the ground
A body mortified with cold.
Stiff and lifeless like a forgotten planet
No thought or opinion through his eyes.

I stood over him, no story could be told
His mind an empty house - silent and still.
Who? Or where? Or why?
No name! Family! Friend!

The wet pavement cradled him first
Before an answer could be found.
The doors were closed, bolted
Drink or drugs or suicide!

Joel Harris (16)
John Cleveland College

METAPHOR POEM

I am a tiger,
I'm always ready to pounce.

I am the colour red,
Always bright and cheerful.

I am a sports car,
Fast and ready to go.

I am a strawberry,
Sweet and full of goodness.

I am the Eiffel Tower,
I liked to be noticed.

I am the country Ibiza,
Ready to party.

I am the sun,
Full of light and happiness.

Andrea Knight (14)
John Cleveland College

METAPHOR POEM

I am a giraffe,
I can reach in high places.

I am a conifer tree,
I'm tall and spiky.

I am the colour yellow,
Bold, bright and always loud!

I am Nelson's Column,
Tall and very colourful.

I am a rake,
Tall, long, really skinny
With spikes on the end.

I am a sunflower,
I never stop growing.

I'm the Empire State Building,
I tower above everyone.

I am a plate of spaghetti,
Long and really stretchy.

Katie King (15)
John Cleveland College

LOSING HER

Tears, never-ending tears cascade down my face,
Knowing that soon, any moment, I could lose her,
The harsh reality of her going ate at my insides,
I thought we had eternity to love one another but I know
                                                    now that is wrong,
Entering the room I gaze at her, how could someone so
                                                    perfect be taken away?
I remember the countless times she wiped away my tears, now
                                                    they were left to fall.
No more hugs, kisses or 'I love you's', nothing would matter anymore.
Tenderly I held her hand, stroked it and told her I loved her,
Deep down thinking it could be the last time to do so.
My memories took me back to happier, cheerful times,
But my memories of the past metamorphosed into sorrowful
                                                    thoughts of the present,
Hope, all I had left was hope that the doctors would be wrong,
Hoping things could be the same again, wanting it to be.
The long pauses between each of her breaths told me it would be soon,
I thought she was beautiful in every way,
Why was it happening? Why should it be her?
The long pause grew longer and longer, she made no sound.
Diminished hope, lost love, even more tears.
I had lost my guide, my safety and most of all -
            My mum.

Samantha Prosser (15)
John Cleveland College

ALL I SEE

Every day I look around
and see what I wish I could be,
I wish I was anything but me.

I see the girl with the perfect face
or the perfect clothes,
Just for one day -

I wish.

I see someone who never gets hurt
by anything or anyone,
I wish I could live like that.

But then I turn
and in a glimpse of a mirror I see,
Everything I wish I would not be.

I see a girl with a distorted face
who seems to have given her life to hurt and pain.
Everything she touches crumbles beneath her.

I see everything *I hate*.

Lindsay James (14)
John Cleveland College

SCHOOL

I go to school every day,
To have a laugh with my friends and play.
The lessons I have are very boring,
It really makes me feel like yawning.

When the clock strikes five past three,
I run straight home to have my tea.
At six o'clock I start my homework,
My little brother starts to annoy me,
Without fail at the same time, same place,
Oh, he is such a jerk!

At ten o'clock I go to bed,
Sometimes I wish I was dead,
Because of the things the teachers have said,
Coursework deadlines run through my head,
All the textbooks I must have read.
They think I am a walking dictionary,
To think of that, to picture me,
They don't have a clue what they see.
They think I am so intelligent and bright,
They think I can get everything right.
But inside I am really afraid,
Of all the exams and revision ahead.

Sarah O'Connor (16)
John Cleveland College

MOMENTS

Moments in the garden.
Moments in the park.
Moments in the light of day.
Moments in the dark.

Seconds by the window.
Seconds by the sea.
Seconds by the man I love,
But he doesn't notice me.

Minutes with my teachers.
Minutes with my work.
Minutes with the bullies.
Minutes with my hurt.

Hours with my mum.
Hours with my dad.
Hours with their fighting,
It really makes me sad.

Days before my holiday.
Days I've got to pack.
Days I leave my friends behind.
Days before we get back.

Weeks of lonely misery.
Weeks of lonely pain.
Weeks of seeing a counsellor,
She takes away my strain.

Years of living my life.
Years of hiding my strain.
Years of trying to have some fun.
Years of giving in to pain.

Maria Bacon (15)
John Cleveland College

METAPHOR POEM

I am cloudy weather,
You don't know
Whether I'm going to rain or shine.

I am a giraffe;
I may be tall but I have good hearing.

I am the Eiffel Tower;
I'm high in the sky.

I am sweet and sour pork,
Sweet, but with a bitter side.

I am white;
I may be plain, but I mix easily.

I am the film 'Boogie Nights',
I like to party wherever I go.

I am an eagle;
I like to soar high in the sky.

I am an oak tree,
Because I'm tall and
Spread out.

I am autumn;
I may not always be sunny
But I'm still warm.

I am a cocktail,
A mixture of different flavours.

Sam Byard (14)
John Cleveland College

METAPHOR POEM

I am a sports car,
Because I'm quick and sporty.

I am the summer's sun,
I'm full of life.

I am blue,
I support Leicester City.

I am an oak tree,
I'm strong.

I am a soft sofa,
I'm soft and gentle.

I am pop music,
I'm very lively.

Robert Hollows (14)
John Cleveland College

MY FRIEND

My little orange Hoover at the bottom of the stairs by the phone,
He talks to me when I'm alone,
Whenever I want to whinge and moan
He's always there by the phone.

My little orange Hoover at the bottom of the stairs by the phone,
When no one else is at home
I sit and watch his orange dome,
I sit and watch him by the phone.

John Pearson (15)
John Cleveland College

METAPHOR POEM

I am a Christmas tree,
Bright and colourful.

I am an office,
Always busy.

I am a rubber,
I try and help erase people's problems.

I am a sun,
Bright and cheerful.

I am dance music,
Loud and energetic.

I am cola,
Fizzy and cool.

I am a Land Rover,
Always live life to the max.

Dana Paton (14)
John Cleveland College

A BUG'S LIFE

A bug in the city with nowhere to go.
Everything's concrete; the bug's feeling low.
It could run, it could hide
But it has too much pride.
All day long he gets into strife
That of course is a 'bug's life!'

Natalie Jones (17)
John Cleveland College

ALL THE WORLD'S A FLOWER

Every person in the world is
merely a flower and all the stages
of life are what a flower will go
through.

First a sprouting little seed
with a little green stem and tiny
roots, only just holding it up,
which needs lots of love and
attention.

Then a stem sprouting bigger
roots to hold it up for when it
grows the leaves of life;
it does this independently as
it is just another part of its
wilting life;
it does not know what to do
and has no one to ask but the
teacher.

Then a devoted plant with
flowers just popping out ready for
the bees to come and take the pollen,
as if ready to share its
first kiss!

Then a big tough plant in full
flower,
trying to survive in the hot
desert-like climate,
sweating like a soldier!

Then the autumn comes and then
the popping of the seeds which fly
away and sprout as they did when
they were only little seeds.

Then the brown old flower which
cannot take any more beating from
the rain from which it used to
thrive on.

And then; dying under the
leaves of the next plant,
it's not to be seen,
it's being trodden on and it's
freezing cold under a blanket of
snow, getting ready to sprout and
live life like this for another
year!

Elizabeth Topp (15)
John Cleveland College

METAPHOR POEM

I am lemonade,
Really fizzy.

I am a lion,
Angered easily.

I am mixed seafood,
Sweet but sour.

I am London Bridge,
I join love and happiness.

I am a conifer,
I go to a point.

I am a fire engine,
Very loud.

Allison Hayton (14)
John Cleveland College

METAPHOR POEM

I am a spade,
I always dig holes for myself.

I am a cat,
When you find me
I will be asleep.

I am a Mini,
I am small
But quick.

I am Egypt,
The sun is always shining for me.

I am Tigger,
I am always full of life.

I am the colour red,
I may be happy,
I may be angry.

Ainsley Lewinsohn (14)
John Cleveland College

METAPHOR POEM

I am a mouse,
Always quiet and very timid.

I am an armchair,
People can always lean on me.

I am a Mini,
Small but very fast.

I am a diamond,
Sparkling and everyone's best friend.

I am a hammer,
I always manage to knock things into place.

I am a lava lamp,
Lively and always on the move.

Michelle Boyd (14)
John Cleveland College

METAPHOR POEM

I am a cat,
Always asleep.

I am chocolate,
Sweet and addictive.

I am summer,
Warm and jolly.

I am Red Bull and vodka,
Very hyperactive.

I am sunshine
Because I'm happy.

I am a bungalow,
Quite small.

I am a rake,
Rather skinny.

Louiz Burrage (14)
John Cleveland College

METAPHOR POEM

I am the colour yellow,
I am always happy.

I am the season of spring,
I am young.

I am a pair of shoes,
I get worn out quickly.

I am sunny weather,
I am cheerful.

I am a chair,
I support people.

I am a peacock,
I am colourful.

I am a necklace,
I like to hang on to things.

Charlotte Woodley (14)
John Cleveland College

METAPHOR POEM

I am a snail;
Very lazy.

I am a fire engine,
Loud and bright.

I am an apple,
Fresh and juicy.

I am a Mercedes,
Fast and classy.

I am an island,
Independent.

I am a cocktail,
Always different.

Laura Bray (14)
John Cleveland College

METAPHOR POEM

I am a lion,
I am big and strong.

I am a doormat,
Everyone wipes their feet on me.

I am yellow,
Always bright.

I am a hammer,
Tough and hardy.

I am the flu,
I make everyone sweat.

I am like an oak tree,
Mature and old.

I am your favourite beer,
You will always come back for more.

Aden Woodhouse (14)
John Cleveland College

METAPHOR POEM

I am a dolphin,
Swimming and playing in the water.

I am a cactus,
Snuggling up
To warm and cosy places.

I am a sports car,
Racing around, fast and furious.

I am a kiwi fruit,
Hard on the outside,
Soft on the inside.

I am Ibiza,
Ready to be wild and party.

I am pasta,
Always bursting with energy.

Rachel Holt (14)
John Cleveland College

METAPHOR POEM

I am the weather,
I am stormy or at peace.

I am a cat,
I like to prowl at night.

I am a building,
I tower above others.

I am a horse,
Strong and quick.

I am a tree,
Waving to people in the breeze.

I am a clock,
Time is in my hands.

Elizabeth Starbuck (14)
John Cleveland College

METAPHOR POEM

I am a bat,
I like to be shrouded
By the night.

I am a clock,
My movement never ceases.

I am a Mini,
Small but ever reliable.

I am sunshine,
Always bright and cheery.

I am a zinnia,
When I wear my colour
People notice me.

I am a palm tree,
I am at my best
In the warmth of the sun.

Katy Lees (14)
John Cleveland College

METAPHOR POEM

I am a swan,
Always moving with grace.

I am a sunflower,
Standing tall and proud.

I am an eye,
Looking out for others.

I am prismatic light,
With varying colours and moods.

I am a library
Brimming with knowledge.

I am a spring landscape,
Fresh and growing.

I am many things
Which is what makes me, me.

Lauren Martin (14)
John Cleveland College

METAPHOR POEM

I am sunny weather,
Always happy.

I am spring,
Nice and cool.

I am a pansy,
Small, skinny and bright.

I am an ice-cream,
Small, sweet and dainty.

I am a cottage,
Small and warm.

I am champagne,
Sweet and sparkling.

Laura Altenhofen (14)
John Cleveland College

A METAPHOR POEM

I am a hyena,
I like to laugh.

I am the colour yellow,
Bright and lively.

I am a Mini car,
I am small but speedy.

I am sugar,
Everyone thinks I'm sweet.

I am a bungalow,
A very level-headed person.

I am a weeping willow,
Emotional but caring.

People call me a rake,
They say I am very slim.

Jenna Short (14)
John Cleveland College

LOST TIME

As she lay there her eyes so serene
I knelt down beside her
More in love than I'd ever been before.
Love started at my temple
It ran, tortured my eyes.
It had reached my trembling fingers
When I realised it was her time.

Blue rapidly merged into black in the shallows of my mind.
The ambulance had arrived
And I wished that it was for me.
They told me to quickly move,
Lifted her frame, heavy and limp.
They strapped her in tight but she wasn't going to move.

Crippled, crying, mourning man,
My dead bride now in the kingdom of above.
Those last three hours had been all the colours of sadness.
The memory is now unclear; my mind's eye blinks and misses it.
The future then was cloudy, conjectural, confusing.
As I looked down at my watch,
I felt her soul through my body, moving.

Garry Payne (16)
John Cleveland College

METAPHOR POEM

I am a hyena,
I'm cheeky and amusing.

I am an oak tree,
I tower up high and am strong and wise.

I am a 4 x 4,
I am strong and reliable.

I am a chisel,
I am sharp
And can stand up to a beating
From the mallet.

I am tuberculosis,
Try all you want but you can't rid
Yourself of me.

I am a drum kit,
As sometimes I am loud.

I am a can of Duff beer,
As you can't get enough
Of the wonderful Duff.

Michael Hemming (14)
John Cleveland College

A CUBE HAS SIX SIDES

I am a beam of torch light,
Shining bright,
But needing to be recharged so I don't shine dim.

A flight of steps am I,
Aiming high,
Always upward,
Resting only when I reach the top.

James Bond's Aston Martin I'd be,
There's more to me,
Than the eye can see,
Deep down inside.

Perhaps a pine tree standing tall,
Treating all,
With honesty and standing straight,
I hope that's me.

I try to be Sir Lancelot,
Rough I am not,
But polite and chivalrous to all whom I trust.

Last of all a Swiss army knife,
Adapted to life.
Made to be versatile
And helpful in every situation.

Hannah Cockburn (14)
John Cleveland College

SPACEMEN

Ten brave spacemen all drinking wine,
One got sucked into a black hole and then there were nine.

Nine cheerful moon-landers drank to celebrate,
One drank too much and then there were eight.

Eight stupid spacemen soaring straight to Devon,
One didn't make it and then there were seven.

Seven silly spacemen, one got in a fix,
Couldn't find the steering wheel so then there were six.

Six lucky spacemen, all of them alive,
One fell in the fuel tank and then there were five.

Five hungry spacemen, one ate something raw,
He got a bad stomach-ache and then there were four.

Four excited spacemen looking at the sea,
One of them lost their way and then there were three.

Three joking spacemen, two of them said, 'Boo!'
Scared the other right off course and then there were two.

Two grumpy spacemen, all their friends had gone,
One killed the other and then there was one.

One sad spacemen, he had just killed John,
He went and committed suicide so then there were none.

Andrew Marshall (15)
John Cleveland College

I AM . . .

I am a Jaguar,
Fast and British.

I am a sandwich,
I have a filling.

I am Rupert the bear,
I like checked shirts.

I am Canary Wharf,
Tall and slender.

I am a shelf,
To hold things up.

I am an itch,
Sometimes annoying.

I am a young oak tree,
I will grow wise and prosperous.

I am a carrot,
Tasty and nocturnal.

I am the sun,
Bright and helping.

I am titanium,
Because I'm protective.

I am a thunderstorm,
Lightning fast,
And unpredictable.

I am me,
Young Daniel.

Daniel Steele (15)
John Cleveland College

What a Night!

My mate and I got a score
But it was stronger than the usual draw.
We thought it was time to have a change
But the little pills looked very strange.

We got ready to go to the club
Instead of going up the pub.
It was going to be a wicked night
Until I got an awful fright.

We popped the pills in the loo
Just as we had planned to.
I felt the pill go down my neck;
I was shaking like an enormous wreck.

Then in the club the place was spinning
And everybody appeared to be grinning.
The room was slowly getting smaller
Whilst all my mates were getting taller.

The pretty lights were speedily flashing;
My head hurt like I'd had a bashing.
In my life I'd never felt so ill,
Just because of a tiny pill.

I woke up in a hospital bed
With tubes and wires coming out of my head.
I could hear my parents loudly crying
And then I heard it, 'I'm afraid she's dying!'

Lisa Farrant (15)
John Cleveland College

METAPHOR POEM

I am the Empire State Building,
Soaring towards the sky.

I am white,
The purest of all colours.

I am a piston,
Back and forth in the same direction.

I am a Porsche 911,
Slinky yet fast.

I am a rock,
Sandstone, a hard exterior yet easy to break.

I am a pair of clear blue eyes,
Beautiful yet essential.

I am clear blue water,
Pure, and good to taste.

Sam Cole (14)
John Cleveland College

METAPHOR POEM

I am a limousine,
Tall, slim and stylish.

I am a giraffe,
Tall and elegant.

I am a vine,
I grow on you and reach for the skies.

I am a skyscraper,
Tall, shiny and good to work with.

I am a chainsaw,
Great as an ally, deadly as an enemy.

I am a cloud,
I wander freely wherever I please.

James Wilkinson (15)
John Cleveland College

METAPHOR POEM

I am a leopard,
Conniving and quick-witted.

I am pine,
Soft on the inside,
Hard and fine on the out.

I am ice-cream,
Refreshing and agreeable
And people always come back for more.

I am gold,
Because I am worth it.

I am a bookcase,
Big and containing much knowledge.

I am a rainbow,
There in a storm,
Bright and beautiful.

Thomas Snelgrove (14)
John Cleveland College

RICHTER FORCE EIGHT

Silently crying in the corner.
The room shook uncontrollably,
Shaking, tumbling down.
What causes such a death,
Such pain and suffering?

No longer here,
No longer alive,
No home, no garden . . .
Nothing.

The shaking has gone;
The tears have vanished:
No more words are spoken.
The pain lingers in the living.
Thinking, continually thinking of the dead.

Emma Rees-Jones (15)
John Cleveland College

I AM . . .

I am a dolphin,
Playful and a strong swimmer.

I am a Rolls Royce,
Stylish and expensive.

I am Mel C,
Sporty and a rock chick.

I am silver,
I shine brighter than others do.

I am Ibiza,
My party goes on all night.

I am wind,
My presence will blow you away.

Kathryn Everton (14)
John Cleveland College

A NEW MILLENNIUM, A NEW BEGINNING?

When Big Ben chimes for the last time
Will all our crimes be left behind,
To die away in the midnight fog
The one that hides us away?

We have heard their desperate cries before,
Rending the air like an Icelandic chill.
Somewhere in our *perfect* world
A child is born to die.

We hold our glasses high in the air:
'Happy New Year' we shout.
Not even caring to think
Of what may be on the brink.

But can we really do as we say,
Change our world for this new day?
Learn to care and share alike
And to put the past to rest at last.

Isabel Toy (15)
John Cleveland College

THE VICARAGE

Clawing at the walls
The ivy creeps.
Suffocating the stone
Quietly; the town sleeps.

Restless spirits are set free
To live out their derelict lives.
The sound of the building
Views past husbands and wives.

Forgotten;
Sadness is absorbed through the walls.
Centuries pass.
To the vicarage eternity calls.

Keira Derbyshire (16)
John Cleveland College

FAMILY

Family can always annoy you
But family will always be there.
Family can always distract you,
But family will always care.

Your family may nag and shout at you
But there will always be one thing
Your family will always care for you
And they will always be loving.

So if you think you don't need them
And that they are always bad.
Remember if one day they were gone,
You would always miss your mum and dad.

Gemma Shepherd (15)
John Cleveland College

THE SEA

The sea is a prancing horse,
Wild, wilful and untamed.
Rearing and roaring onto the rocky shore,
Thundering hooves and flattened ears:
The storm clouds gather.

The waves grow higher and stronger still,
Charging forward, jumping high,
Eyes aflame and mane a-flowing:
Will this tempest ever wane?

The sea is calm, the storm's abating,
The undulating motions of his swift raven mane.
Is he tamed, or is he sleeping?
Will the next tide see his waking?

Jennifer Harvey (15)
John Cleveland College

THE MATCH

Saturday at last,
3 o'clock is the time.
For the roar of the crowd,
The thump of the ball on the boot,
The grunt as the player heads the ball.
The whistle for a foul,
Abuse given to the referee.
The ball is hit
The keeper dives
The back of the net rustles with the movement.
The match is won!

Richard Donnachie (15)
John Cleveland College

INCOGNITO

Crying inside,
Screaming out loud;

You just can't hear it!

Apathetic towards life's meaning:
Oblivious towards self-meaning.
Deaf to words of wisdom
Wise to words that impair.

Empty inside
Emotions too deep;
Wounds that are too deep to heal.
Scarred
Yet invisibly.

Justice is yet to be carried out:
As the innocent suffer,
The guilty laugh out loud,
Yet others are too blind to see it.

How?

How can he do this to me?
Why did she walk out on me?
The equation's uneven;
It just doesn't balance out.

Charlene Richardson (16)
John Cleveland College

CLASSIFIED

My face is a mask,
Devoid of all emotion.
I am solitary,
Hidden.
Outside I may look like a bubbling spring:
Inside I am a well of sadness.
One day my secret will rise to the surface,
Because I am a dam
And the pressure is too much
I am going to shatter
Out of control
Or remain a mystery,
Classified information
That everybody wants access to?
They ask for 'The Truth'
But if they *knew*
I know
I would be avoided -
'Like the plague'

Their curiosity grows
And I become evermore popular.
I'm popular *because* I'm different
And mysterious . . .
They think they know who I am
But they don't really know at all
I am a gypsy.

Maria Jackson (15)
John Cleveland College

THE CRASH

Flying over the north Atlantic
On our way home
The plane's engines die down.
What is going on?

The captain's voice is heard on the tannoy
Telling us of problems he has found.
People begin to panic,
Holding onto their loved ones.

We drop through the thick cloud;
The sea is really close.
There is no land in sight.
Will we live or die?

After we hit the ocean,
The plane floats for a while.
Many people are injured,
Some are even dead.

Survivors cram into the life-rafts
With the crew taking command.
The plane finally goes under
With people still on board.

Years later, people still ask
To hear our tragic story.
Their mouths drop and their eyes widen
Unwilling to believe.

Gary Betts (16)
John Cleveland College

WHEN THE WEIGHT UPON MY SHOULDERS . . .

When the weight upon my shoulders,
is too much for me to bear
and I feel like I can't go on
I get down on my knees in prayer.

My eyes have been opened
to the world and all its wrongs.
I don't want to look anymore;
with my family I belong.

Sometimes I feel sorrow;
it's deep within my soul.
I know I should not feel too bad
about some things I can't control.

God is always there to guide me,
with every step I take;
He cares, loves and teaches me,
through all achievements and mistakes.

Laura Davey (15)
John Cleveland College

PARENTS, HEY!

I just sit down
I've just got home
And all at once, they start to moan.

Wash the dishes
Make the tea
Why do they always groan at me?

I spend all day at school
And all night at work.
Do they never think my feet might hurt?

But day after day it's always the same,
Parents, hey!
Who else to blame?

Michelle Styles (16)
John Cleveland College

THE SEA

A huge octopus with tentacles galore,
Dolphins, crabs and lots, lots more,
A beautiful mermaid with long golden hair,
Swims gracefully about without a care.
Seaweed grows on the seabed,
Some are green and some bright red,
long slimy eels
and cute little seals,
pearl white coral
and crabs that quarrel.
Small dainty seahorse and elegant whales,
Umbrella-like jellyfish wobbly and pale.

Krupa Trivedi (11)
Loughborough High School

REVERIE

Sitting by the window on a stifling summer's day
My thoughts become distorted
Classroom drifting into dreams.
The scene begins to blur,
The phenomena all one.
In the clearing all alone,
The evil round me makes its presence known.
Cruel winds begin to blow,
The burning summer heat, now icy cold.
Leaves fall from the trees,
Tarnished garments on the ground
Corpses standing all about.
The clearing is a dungeon,
Prisoners of the night.
Whistling wind gives forth an icy chill.
I rise upon the wind while gliding like a leaf
Looking down on treetops at the silent world below.
Leaves are made to rustle by the creatures of the night.
Owls crying, hunting for their prey.
Returning to the clearing,
Smoke spirals to the heavens.
Fear is all around.
Fire is licking at the gnarled tree-stumps.
Transforming trees to candelabra,
A visage of the sun.
I lift my eyes, am dazzled by the sun.
The fire's heat, the classroom's heat are both becoming one.
Sitting by the window on a stifling summer's day,
My thoughts become distorted
Classroom drifting into dreams.

Imogen Mitchell (12)
Loughborough High School

LIVING ON MARS

It's the twenty-first century
I'm living in space.
Now Mars is home
To the whole human race.

How Earth ended
I must explain.
The world was destroyed
By acidic rain.

Now we have
Metallic trees.
That sway in the wind
In a rusty breeze.

The grass is of copper
The bushes of lead
And every animal
Is starving or dead.

We race around
In supersonic cars.
On this planet
That we call Mars.

The future is good
And sometimes sad.
Sometimes happy.
Sometimes bad.

Sally Robinson (11)
Loughborough High School

NIGHTMARE!

Tossing and turning
Mind is whirling
Fire is burning
Light is twirling.
Falling deep
Drowning in sleep
Reality fades
Monstrous shades.
Running away
Caught as prey
Never ending
Life is bending.
Axe comes down
Beginning to drown
Ice cold
No hold
Going under
Clap of thunder
Scream out loud
Lost in a crowd.
Closing in
Full of sin
Evil and dark
Sound of a lark.
Brings to life
Free from the knife
I'm awake!

Katie Gotheridge (13)
Loughborough High School

NIGHTMARE

Falling, falling
Over and over,
Tumbling, tumbling
Head over heels.

Knowing, knowing
If I keep on going,
My feet will slip from me
Like slippery eels.

I have this nightmare
I used not to care,
But now, to go to bed
I do not dare.

If I keep on falling
While I'm still asleep,
If I hit the bottom
My life I will not keep.

If this nightmare
Will haunt me forever,
I'll always go on falling
Over and over.

Hannah Thomas (12)
Loughborough High School

MY PET

I had a hamster named Toby
Who I loved very much
He lived in a cage
And not in a hutch.

He was soft to touch
And cream and white.
He slept all day
And stayed awake all night.

He loved to play
Or roll in his ball.
Through the lounge
And up the hall.

He had a small round nose
And big black eyes.
And then one day
He said 'Bye, bye!'

He lay in his cage
His life had come to an end.
We all loved him dearly
And he was my best friend.

Eloise Macrow (11)
Loughborough High School

LIFE IN THE FUTURE

As I walk through the gates of the futuristic school,
I see a large metal structure
Rising high into the dazzling blue sky.
There are square blocks and round blocks
All with huge plate glass windows.
Revealing a school alien yet familiar.

The girls in their metallic leather uniforms,
Their black skirts and white tops,
Patterned with glittering studs.
Sit like models at small round steel tables,
With only a control panel in front of them.
Its lights shining like Christmas trees,
Their fingers poised ready to answer a question,
At the touch of a button.

The teacher on a small platform at the front of the classroom,
Fixes her glaring eyes on one of her pupils.
Her head is square and sits on a box-shaped body.
The rays of light from the windows reflect in all directions.
No words come out of her mouth,
The lessons flash up on an electronic board behind her.
She is of course a Robot!

Kirsty Godrich (11)
Loughborough High School

MY DREAMLAND

When it's time to go to sleep I look forward
to going to bed.
For I go to the place where I only go
and magic fills my head.

And when I start to drift away I go to a
different land,
A land which is enchanting and I call this
my own dreamland.

The fields are full with golden wheat and the sky
is as blue as blue,
The bright green trees stand proud and tall
and the grass is fresh with dew.

The vivid rare creatures jump with joy, while the
little frogs jump in the air.
My dreamland is a wonderful place, for everything
there is equal and fair.

But then I have to leave my land because morning
is drawing near,
And the sun is shining in the sky for another
day of the year.

Meghan Jarvis (12)
Loughborough High School

DREAMS AND NIGHTMARES!

I walk in green meadows,
Although I never leave my bed.
I swim in the sea
Although I never get wet.
I fly high in the sky
Although my feet stay on the ground.
I do this whilst sleeping
As it goes on in my head.

I meet my superstar hero
Although I'm not in Hollywood.
I go to Barbados
Without having to step into a plane.
I go walking on the moon
Without travelling in a rocket.
I do this whilst sleeping
As it goes on in my head.

I dance in front of millions,
Although I never move my feet.
I star in a blockbuster movie
Although I never move my lips.
I even win millions on the lottery
Although I never buy a ticket.
I do this whilst sleeping
As it goes on in my head.

However, there's another side to dreams,
Which is black and pretty dismal.
Spiders, wolves, ghosts and monsters,
Creatures I don't recognise.
All around me creeping
Getting ready for the kill.
Glinting eyes appearing in the darkness
Staring out and far beyond.

Where teachers give you whippings
And your families die.
And you wake up with tears
Streaming down your face.
However, you are not at all awake
In fact, your nightmare is continuing,
Getting worse, stage by stage,
And however hard you try, you just can't wake up.

Whether a dream
Or a nightmare.
It happens when you're sleeping.
When your head rests on the pillow,
And your eyes are tightly closed.
However, when your parents come to wake you up
And it's time to go to school
Your dreams are left behind, until you go to sleep again.

Kim Humby (12)
Loughborough High School

FIRE

Hot, blazing, burning fire
Hissing and spitting its scorching flame.
It destroys everything it can,
Catching it in its smoky cage.
It crackles through the day and night
Not going out without a fight.

The treacherous flame scalds its enemy
Leaving it dazzled and lifeless.
When will it stop its evil ways?
Can it be tamed and give us warmth and light?
This we will find out, in the dead of the night.

Lucy Corbett (11)
Loughborough High School

A Dream

I lay in bed, a pillow over my head,
My eyes feel heavy, my legs like lead.
The television's blaring in the living room
Echoing round the house with a deafening boom.
My brother is screaming in his cot,
I can't get to sleep hearing this lot.
I toss and turn and start to doze,
And eventually my eyes close . . .

I discover myself on a sunlit beach.
Hearing the seagulls above me screech.
I dabble my feet into the cool blue sea,
I hear the water calling me.
I feel awake, alert, alive.
I bend my knees and jump up to dive.
I find myself flying through the air
Scattering birds here and there.
I fly past bright twinkling stars,
Circling Jupiter, Saturn and Mars.
Starting to fall, I reach for a line
And find myself swinging from vine to vine.
In the jungle where parrots fly into view
The colours of the rainbow, red, yellow, green and blue.
I swing, but miss a nearby vine
And find myself on a ship drinking wine.
I take a sip and spit it out
Nearby I hear someone shout.
I try to run to the side of the ship
But at that point, the boat starts to tip.
The water gets nearer, nearer, nearer.
I see the world a whole lot clearer.
And with a splash I land at last
On the soft seabed, where the fish swim past.

A fish's head starts to swell
It reminds me of someone I know so well.
It opens its mouth with a stream of clear bubbles,
And out comes a voice which I know means trouble . . .

'Wake up! Wake up!' my mother shouts.
'You're going to be late, you'd better get out!'
And with a groan I climb out of bed
My eyes are heavy, my legs like lead.

Emma Flynn (12)
Loughborough High School

ENGLISH

I've got to learn my vocab
Remember that verb.
Don't forget punctuation
Do well in comprehension.
Get better on letters
Don't forget my commas.
Remember those spellings
I'm very hardworking.
Oh, I really wish
I really wish
I was good at English.
I've got to separate normal nouns
From pronouns.
Stories are imaginative,
Find the objective.
Oh I really wish
I really wish
I was good at English.

Vanessa Hayter (11)
Loughborough High School

THE NIGHTMARE!

'Where am I?' I screamed, my heart pounding with fear.
My bed, my room was nowhere near.
Devilish laughter haunting my face.
This world that I saw was a different place.
I looked around and I could see
Mysterious figures approaching me.
Their faces lit up with a strange kind of glow.
Who or what they were, I still do not know.
A loud laugh echoed in the air,
I turned round; but nothing was there.
Below my feet, the ground began to shake,
The figures came nearer, but there was no escape.
I froze in horror, unable to yell.
I was positive that this must be hell.
I woke up shivering, my heart beating fast
And lay back down, in peace at last.

Pamela Swallowe (12)
Loughborough High School

THE DREAMS OF THE NIGHT

Darkness spreads across the sky;
The dreams of the night swirling around.
Emotions are carried: sadness or joy?
What fantasy or tragedy have I found?

The distorted images in my head,
What puzzle will I have to solve?
Who will I meet, where will I go?
The mystery will now unfold.

Nightmare strikes; a whirl of gloom,
A shiver runs down my spine.
I can't run away, I'm trapped in despair,
But when I wake all will be fine.

I'm floating in my fantasy,
The pleasure found deep inside.
I want to stay hovering above,
But all things have to subside.

Becky Newman (12)
Loughborough High School

ON THE TRAIN

The horn sounded, we were on our way.
Slowly we started, being pushed and parted.
Gathering speed, frightened horses darted,
Then all of a sudden, the train started jumping
We had changed to a main line and the steam was pumping.
The crash of the tracks as we cleared the junction,
We sped through the tunnel dark and bare,
No lights for a second, then a sudden glare.
Billows of steam, a crash and a crack
Ended the tunnel by the side of a shack.
The brakes squealed and squeaked as we stopped at the station.
Birds flew off, with children in jubilation.
The end of the journey, what a busy day
All quiet now, just a prrrr away.

Rebecca Smith (11)
Loughborough High School

DREAM FLIGHT

I only had twelve pages to go!
Would Concorde fly freely or fall steeply?
Before I had time to answer this question,
I was becoming tired and very sleepy.

I drifted off into a different world,
It was warm and beautifully green,
The grass was long, wavy and soft,
It was peaceful and serene.

As I looked round I realised,
I was flying through the sky.
I soared over chimneys and trees
Flying, flying high.

In the distance, a splash of blue,
Next to me a hovering bird.
All around clean, whooshing air,
Below fields, a black and white cow herd.

Now the splash of blue became,
A great big, blue sea.
Of sparkling, crystal clear waves,
And dolphins swimming free.

Everything disappeared.
What was going on?
I looked around my room
To find my dream had gone!

Georgina Riley (12)
Loughborough High School

MOTHER EARTH

Mother Earth looked in the mirror
'I look like a wreck!' she said.
Where there had been an ozone layer
There was a bald patch instead.

There used to be crystal clear oceans
Splashing around her head.
Now they are black and poisoned
With rubbish on the seabed.

Humans crawling over her skin
She thought of them as lice.
She wished that she could get rid of them
Just like they killed rats and mice.

When she took a breath
She found it hard, with hardly any woods.
The towns' pollution makes her cough
And it doesn't look too good.

When she looks at the other planets
She sees those more beautiful than her.
With no humans to wreck their surface
She finds it hard to bear.

They did not make her mistake
They did not let anything live.
For at first she thought it would be give and take
But then, she learned, just give.

Lucy Ann Colwill (12)
Loughborough High School

THE COMPUTER

The computer is like a human,
But without a soul or life,
It has no feelings,
Plus no heart.

The computer has a purpose,
It has a mind of its own,
It doesn't have any skin,
It doesn't have any bone.

The computer is here to serve us,
It always obeys our commands,
It never tells a lie,
It never has any demands.

The computer is a useful machine,
It can always do our will,
Even though the Internet,
May cost you a very large bill!

The computer isn't an individual,
It hasn't a mom or dad,
But it is a part of our family,
And we are all very glad.

Claire Bayley (11)
Loughborough High School

THE WHITE GHOST

As the white ghost treads on solid ground,
Its long tail sways with elegance from side to side.
It runs with pure grace, and makes no sound but the
Soft whisper of his neigh.

He wants to break free, but he can't
He wants to live his own life, but he can't
He wants to do what he wants, but he can't

Alone and afraid he waits for a lonely passer-by
Who will pamper him.
Love him, show affection to him
But that will never happen.

His nose as soft as velvet
His foot as hard as rock.
His mane as thin and delicate as baby's skin.
His eyes as dark and unhappy as an endless pit.

As the years trail on by
The white ghost becomes old and weak.
And as the mist covers the land
You can still hear the faint whisper
Of the white ghost.

Fay Collinson (11)
Loughborough High School

DREAMS AND NIGHTMARES

Dozing away, you slowly fall into a sweet slumber,
Racing thoughts turn around in your head.
Every thought tries to become a dream.
A story about a beautiful scene.
Maybe a dream in which you can fly,
Soaring in an endless sky.

After a while the dream you're enjoying,
Now turns to a dream which is more annoying
Death and unhappy thoughts swarm in your head.

Nice visions drowned out in the muddle of sleep,
In the dream where you fly, you end in a heap.
Ghosts and ghouls, monsters and Dinosaurs,
Hawks attacking with their claws.
Though you struggle you cannot get free,
Monsters throw you in the sea.
A big splash! But what happens next?
Relief, that I feel when I'm out of danger, and
Everyone is no longer a stranger
Something that we will never know . . . is why we dream
and imagine so.

Rachel Adcock (12)
Loughborough High School

THERE'S BLOOD UPON THE SNOW . . .

There's blood upon the snow
And fur hangs on the breeze.
A trail of paw prints go
In amongst the trees.

The panting of the throat,
The lolling of the tongue.
The snow upon the coat,
The howling wolfpack's song.

Hoofbeats pound like drums
Galloping through the wood.
The caribou's pulse thrums,
As the wolves bay for blood.

The caribou slumps and falls
Like a broken doll.
The wolfpack howls and calls
They always take their toll.

Danielle Frisby (14)
Loughborough High School

FUTURE VOICES

I lay asleep in bed and thought,
I with a million voices fought.
I hear them calling out for me,
I hear the sound of the lapping sea,
And suddenly I am lying there,
Surrounded by many children fair.
It is the year 3008,
And the world is filled with pain and hate,
These are the children of the future,
And never have I seen such sad children cuter.
I realise the world must not get like this,
We must all listen to that quiet voice, that little hiss.
I wake up in my bed again,
I vow to prevent those children's pain,
If I could I'd be an adult in their time,
But as it is I must reach you with my rhyme,
Please listen and heed,
For you have heard the great need,
I've vowed it once and I'll vow it again,
I vow to ease those children's pain.

Joanna Davey (12)
Loughborough High School

DREAMS

Smoothly passing
Like being whisked through air.
Calm and gentle as if you were really there.
Happy thoughts, nothing bad comes to mind,
All happening as if it was true.
Simple things just made so extravagant.

Down, down, down
Just like a falling star.
Lightly passing in such a plain tone.
In a dream, people never have a reason to moan.
Life so simple just with no complications,
Happiness is the key to everything.

This world is filled with cherubims
Who can do no wrong.
Gliding, swerving, jumping
Landing on a soft pillow,
Quilted and embroidered with gold.
You really could be any age, young or old.

A fantasy for everyone
To enjoy such a wonderful experience.
Further, further, down I go.
I want to stay with the happy people.
Oh, what a smooth ride
How I wish it could last forever.

Faster, faster, down I go
I can feel the wind behind me.
Oh how I miss my beautiful pillow.
Gliding smoothly, so fast as if it were make-believe.
I reached the bottom of my wondrous flights.
What happens next? I will never know.

Victoria Brown (13)
Loughborough High School

HANDHELD SECRETS

Unspoken feelings, silent thoughts,
Uncharted dreams, inspired wants.
Corners filled with empty visions
Locked away in a thousand prisons.

Galaxies filled with leaden stars,
A future that I want for ours.
A labyrinth formed by a wondered tear
That trickles down when you're not near.

Reflections in a phoney mirror
Feigned by spirits from my fear.
Drifting as a floating bubble
Burst by pains that cause this trouble.

Hands that flail about through bars,
A happiness that loving mars.
Images shattered to broken glass
What I saw, I never asked.

Needs that burn in angry fires
Covered up by crossing wires.
In you, the power to turn a key
To turn this madness away from me.

An oblong compass to help you see,
Navigate worlds unknown to me.
Bullets shot from blazing suns
A shroud of non-existent guns.

Lives of rips and fragmentation
Years of built-up adoration.
Handheld secrets you share too
A distance closed from me to you.

Nicola Simpson (15)
Loughborough High School

MY DREAM

I have a dream that one day:
No matter who they are, or what they are
everyone should be treated as equals.
I have a dream that one day:
The words poverty and homelessness will
have no meaning.
I have a dream that one day:
Each person has the same opportunities
as the next.
I have a dream that one day:
That wars are a thing of the past, and that
not one person on Earth would think of
starting one.
I have a dream that one day:
Guns, bombs and missiles will be banished
from our land.
I have a dream that one day:
Friends would be friends and they would never
lie or cheat one another, but, be honest and trust
each other.
I have a dream that one day:
Each person will feel loved and cared for.
I have a dream that one day:
For each animal to be treated as every living
thing,
I have a dream that one day:
That there will be no pollution and we shall breathe in
fresh air wherever we are in the world.

Fiona Wemyss (12)
Loughborough High School

A FUTURE VOICE

A future voice is a voice
That has not been heard.

If you were to wake
In a year far from now
Would you find a world
Full of sadness and pain
That cannot be cured?

A future voice is a voice
That has not been heard.

If you were to wake
In a year far from now
Would you find a world
Full of laughter and joy
Without lies or sorrow?

A future voice is a voice
That has not been heard.

If you were to wake
In a year far from now
Would you find a world
Full of smoke, dirt and pollution
With the smell of petrol
Hanging in the air?

A future voice is a voice
That has not been heard.

Alex Sear-Mayes (11)
Loughborough High School

IF ONLY . . .

Emily's lucky
She's been told to stay inside at break.
I wish I had a bad cold!
But I'm sure I'll get one at this rate!

Emma's lucky
She only got one in her maths test.
I wish I had to stay inside
And learn all the rest!

My teacher's lucky
At break she drinks tea in the *staffroom*
I wish I was a teacher! (at break only).

Every day it's the same
The sky is grey
The air is cold
The snow is thick
There's a cloudy sky.
The clouds are full of water waiting to burst,
And yet the teachers still say

'Go out and get some fresh air!'

Well it's all right for them, they're inside.
It's never-ever me who gets told to stay inside.
In the warmth with the radiators and the
Confined spaces to snuggle up in.
If only it was me who could stay inside,
Instead of being stuck outside here in the
Freezing cold!

Miriam Louise Gindy (12)
Loughborough High School

MY GHOSTLY SPIRIT

I was alone one day,
Far, far away,
Didn't know which way to turn,
Alone, away, I began to yearn.
I was frightened,
I tightened,
I played with my curls,
I kept seeing whirls,
A real spiral in my head,
I kept wishing I was in my bed.
I then stood up all alone,
I saw a bone.
I couldn't believe my eyes,
I kept seeing me saying my byes.
I knew something was wrong,
I kept hearing the song.
My head kept spinning,
I felt myself dropping . . .
Down, down and down.
Is that a clown?
I looked up scared,
I saw a face looking weird.
'Get up my dear child, get up.'
I looked up . . .
Once again my imagination had gone too far.

Laura Morris (11)
Loughborough High School

SEASON WEEKS

Blossoms are falling on Monday,
On Tuesday it's nice and warm,
It's very sweet smelling on Wednesday,
On Thursday we're caught in a storm.
It rains on and off on Friday,
On Saturday it is clear,
On Sunday it is the end of spring,
And summer is very near.

It's very hot on Monday,
On Tuesday we go to the beach,
It rains a lot on Wednesday,
Thursday we get an ice-cream each.
On Friday ice-creams have sold out,
On Saturday there is a short drought,
On Sunday, autumn's about.

It's cold and quite wet on Monday,
On Tuesday the leaves start to fall,
Everything's hectic on Wednesday,
On Thursday we find the frost cruel.
On Friday the garden's neglected,
Saturday, a hedgehog's detected,
On Sunday, winter's expected.

It snows a lot on Monday,
On Tuesday I get cold feet,
It gets a bit warmer on Wednesday,
On Thursday it begins to sleet.
Everything freezes on Friday,
On Saturday the snow starts to go,
On Sunday it gets much warmer,
And spring begins to show.

Gillian James (11)
Loughborough High School

NOTHING

Nothing is silent,
Nothing is there.
Nothing is invisible,
But nobody cares.

Nothing is a person,
Nothing is a beast.
It creeps around behind you,
Just to say the least.

Nothing has no one to talk to,
Nothing has no friends.
Nothing will be on its own,
It'll never end.

Nothing wants to be with you,
Nothing wants to talk.
Nothing wants to run with you,
Nothing wants to walk.

Nothing is a lonely soul,
Nothing stands and stares.
Nothing moves along the wall,
It creeps up the stairs.

Nothing is forgiven,
If it does any wrong.
Nothing has no words to speak,
No voice to sing a song.

Nothing has happiness,
Nothing has sadness too.
Nothing can not laugh or cry,
Nothing needs you.

Sarah Oatley (11)
Loughborough High School

JEALOUSY

It is dusk.
I creep around the house I dream for.
Inside is my lucky brother,
Surrounded by his family.
He has a job.
He has friends.
He has family,
While I am all on my own,
He knows that.
But he doesn't care.
This hatred burns inside me.
I plan for him to die,
And me to take his place.
This is all happening inside my keen and sickening mind.
I want that life.
I deserve it.
Anger is burning inside me.
Like molten lava
My life is in ruins.
I live in indignation.
Suddenly I hear a noise.
A dog is barking.
I duck below the window,
And try to creep away,
But they have already spotted me.
They know I shall return one day.

Amy Aitkenhead (11)
Loughborough High School

VOICES AND CHOICES

They once had future voices,
They helped me to make choices.
Mandela said to accept blacks,
He said to believe them,
Understand and follow their tracks.
I believed in him and them.
>They once had future voices,
>They helped me to make choices.
Neil took his small paces,
Yet they were giant leaps,
Down on Earth he is admired by many faces,
I believed in them.
>They once had future voices,
>They helped me to make choices.
Fleming, Lister and Pasteur,
Advanced the fight against disease,
Their knowledge helps us thrive and prepare,
I believed in them.
>They once had future voices,
>They helped me to make choices.
John, George, Ringo and Paul,
Lit up the world with their music
Their words are still sung and taught,
People believed in them.
>They once had future voices,
>They helped me to make choices.

Olivia Pay (11)
Loughborough High School

TIME MACHINE

I sit in the corner of a dark, dark, room
waiting for a person to come.
After waiting for what seemed a lifetime,
a light is turned on.

Had my wish come true?
A child is approaching me
A child can't steer me,
I am too great, I will twist and turn,
He will not stand it.

> I am a time machine,
> time travelling is what I do
> anyone who climbs on board
> sees the world the way I do.

He steps in and closes the door.
He's in for a bumpy ride.
He doesn't know what he has got himself into.
He'd better hold on tight.

He dials the year 2006,
he will get a shock,
The world is empty,
meaningless and dirty.

The little boy is full of guilt,
Feels he should have looked,
after the world better.

> I am a time machine,
> time travelling is what I do
> anyone who climbs on board
> learns a thing or two.

Sophie Waite (11)
Loughborough High School

I HAVE A DREAM

I have a dream
That one day;
I'll own a horse
And it'll be bay.

I have a dream
That one day;
I'll be an actress
Famous and gay.

I have a dream
That one day;
I'll be a singer
Come what may.

I have a dream
That one day;
To travel the world
And fly away.

I have a dream
That one day;
I'll be a mother
I hope and pray.

I have a dream
That one day;
To be a grandmother
Old and grey.

I have a dream
That one day;
To rule the world,
You *must* obey!

Anne Pentecost (11)
Loughborough High School

VOICES OF THE FUTURE

Visions of bio-genetic engineering
Unsure, unknown entities
Seeds grown on the laboratory floor
Struggling forms of thrashing flesh
Given life where once was death
Irradiated masses of squamous cells
Remnants of the genome project
Reasons for living
Lonely orphan
Life without love
Hope without pain
Needing but not wanting
Striving but never reaching
Crying without tears
Laughing but not smiling
Grasping the world, your tiny fingers
Holding the key
Test tube trials
Tragedy's child
Forced into life
Timeless creature
Baby without mother's womb
Child of the future
Voice of the future
Created by the voices of your past
Silent echoes of your heritage
Millennium brain child
Master of the universe
Voices of the future
Silently screaming.

Maryam Rejai-Moghadam (11)
Loughborough High School

SCHOOL BULLIES

It's not fair, it's not fair,
Why do they always pick on me?
Why me? Why me?
The bus arrives,
My heart is pounding.
Why is it me they're always threatening?
I get on the bus,
I sit near the back,
Oh no! Here comes Zac,
He's coming closer,
I'm moving away,
This is another terrible day,
He sits in front,
He has an evil look,
I hide myself behind a book,
The bus stops,
I get off,
Oh no! Here comes Zac's friend Geoff,
He walks towards me,
My hands are trembling,
My brains aren't working.
'Hand over your chocolate bar,' he grunts,
I handed it over and sighed,
Suddenly he held it up high!
I wanted to show him that I was not short,
I leapt up high, but no use at all,
I thought of basketball, I thought of netball,
But nothing can stop me from being
small,
I want to be tall! I want to be tall!
But with no luck at all.

Jennifer Cheung (11)
Loughborough High School

FUTURE VOICES

I wish I could meet a rock star,
or maybe a scientist,
In the future maybe I will.
I might meet aliens who talk like teletubbies,
Dinosaurs who destroy the world,
Ghosts who tell my future,
Monkeys who dance like balloons,
Anything could happen in the future.
I might turn into the biggest mouse,
Or the loudest aeroplane.
Maybe taller than the Eiffel Tower,
All these things are my imagination,
I see talking gorillas,
Snakes with legs, arms and noses.
I see mice who fly around the world,
Elephants that are the lightest animals in the world,
I see the sun raining,
Rainbows that are black,
Children that are good,
Free chocolates and sweets,
Houses that are free,
Chocolate streams and ice-creams,
I see friendships that last forever,
And children that are cleverer than adults,
This is my imagination of the future.

Joanna Ackling (12)
Loughborough High School

FUTURE VOICES

I hear the future voices,
I hear them night and day,
I hear the future voices,
And they say
You are my mother,
You are my daughter,
You are my sister,
You are my aunt,
I hear my children shout and scream,
'I shan't, I shan't, I shan't.'
I think I'm scared of dying,
But really I am not sure.
I wonder what life is like in heaven
Did God mean there would be war?
I woke up once again lying in my bed,
I wonder whether these voices will ever be out of my head.
I wonder whether I will ever have children,
Or be a mother, a daughter or an aunt.
All that I know is
I shall or I shan't.
These voices are forever,
And forever they will be.
In my mind and in my thoughts,
And belong to no one but me.

Lauren Powley (11)
Loughborough High School

RACING TO NEW YORK

Gigantic sleek ship,
Cutting through black water,
All was calm and quiet,
Band playing soft soothing, sophisticated music,
Couples dancing,
People chatting and laughing,
Titanic racing to New York.

Engines roaring,
Churning, throbbing, thudding,
Smoke billowing,
Titanic racing to New York.

Iceberg!
Menacing, glistening, glittering blue,
People frantically running screaming and shouting,
Titanic not racing to New York.

Children crying and squealing,
Clinging desperately onto their parents,
People pushing and shoving,
Titanic not racing to New York.

Quiet and calm again,
Except for muffled cries and sobs,
And the slap of the oars of the lifeboats.
Titanic slipping to a watery grave.

Kate Smith (11)
Loughborough High School

MY FEELINGS ON CHILD ABUSE

I draw back my curtain and see
A world rocked by hate and clasped by fear.
Emotions bottling up until the cork bursts,
I see the forlorn eyes of our children.
      Perplexed. Frustrated
      Bewildered. Wretched.
For their eyes can tell a story,
A story of hatred, revulsion, anger and fear,
Their tiny, fragile bodies reveal secrets.
      Bruised. Battered
      Abused. Frail.
These secrets are dark, sinister and haunting,
For they tell of a bleak and frigid world.
This is a world I don't like, it's unreal.
      Helpless. Homeless
      Hopeless. Unloved.
For I see in every neighbourhood, every town,
A nation of child abusers,
Why do we subject children to such cruelty?
      Children are our future,
      Your future. The future.
Children are not punchbags, they deserve rights,
So don't close the curtain in disgust,
Campaign for a brighter future.
      Child abuse.
      Must stop now.

Jenny Morgan (11)
Loughborough High School

WHEN WILL WE LEARN?

When will we learn?
Only when it is too late.
Only when the last tree,
Has been turned into tomorrow's
Fish and chip papers, or into
A cute little birthday greeting.

Only when the last river's
Innocent, sparkling flow
Has been turned into a
Seething, polluted, dirty
Mass, and its life is lying
On the shore, its spirit gone,
Forever.

Only when the last breath
Of fresh, clean air has
Been pushed aside by
Deadly fumes, and made
Unpure by the mark factories
Leave, high in the air.

Only then will we learn,
Only when it is too late.

Katie Rowe (12)
Loughborough High School

CATS

Cats have soft and dainty paws,
but hidden away are razor claws.
Claws don't look like they can scratch,
but really, there just is no match.
Their pink tongues seem so cute, I know,
but tongues hide teeth that do not show.
They might lick you, indeed they might,
but don't forget that they can bite!

Soft and smooth, the fur they groom,
sprawled on a chair, taking the room.
They purr so loud it seems just like
a lawnmower is taking flight!
Their whiskers sprout from chubby cheeks,
and big, green eyes don't look so meek.
Ears turn round to locate sounds,
and noses sniff at what surrounds.

Cats have different coloured coats,
There are ten colours at the most.
Some are ginger, some are black,
some have white lines down their back.
Some are misty grey or blue,
some are multi-coloured too.
Cats will just sit in your lap.
Or they only let you pat.

Lucy May Louise Usher (11)
Loughborough High School

THERE'S A VOICE

Listen there's a voice inside
Telling you the way to go,
Listen it's shouting out at you
No, no, no!

Do you listen to that voice?
Or only think of pride?
Later on you will wonder
Was that right?

'Help me!'
You hear it cry.
'Help, or I may die.'
Do you stand and help?
Or do you run and hide?

If you don't listen to this voice
Forever it's inside,
It will harm your conscience,
It will take your pride.

One day in your long-lived life
You will understand,
It will help you get along,
You could have changed the land.

When you take your final breath,
Conscience stays beside.
Listen there's a voice inside,
Telling you the way to go,
Listen to it, it will change your life,
For good? Who knows.

Alice Gee (11)
Loughborough High School

STAND

Arise, get up, or be upstanding,
Stand up; set, place, up end.
Survive, endure, tolerate and abide,
Last through, suffer, bear,
From the word . . .

Prevail, remain, persist or apply,
Stand by; support, defend, uphold,
Affirm confirm, wait and maintain,
Adhere to, obtain, continue,
From the word . . .

Resign, quit, step aside or withdraw,
Stand for; symbolise, represent, signify,
Mean, illustrate, refer to and sponsor,
Promote, advocate, second
From the word . . .

Replace, relieve, or cover for,
Stand out; prominent, conspicuous, noticeable,
Protrude, project, stick out, and extend,
Bulge, jut out, overhang,
From the word . . .

Confront, brave, challenge, or dispute,
Stand up to; question, resist, defy,
Position, attitude, stance and policy,
Philosophy, belief, sentiment,
From the word . . .

Stand

Suzanne Bryan (15)
Loughborough High School

A WEARY MOTHER UPON HER SON'S FALL FROM GRACE

Successfully you were tempted by Mars,
In vain you struggle, in naivety to
Explain your valid reasoning but,
In truth you know there is no excusing your mistake,
Your mutinous insurrection.
Can you see your reflection
When you sit admiring yourself near the lake?
Or are you transparent as the mocking expression that you wear?
You declare you do not care,
I know you better, I know how much you hurt,
I know where your heel is, Achilles.
I try to avoid it. I have no need to cause you pain.
I only want you to comprehend how you hurt me.
It would be a relief to despise you,
But I love you too much.
I often stay silent,
Ignoring your violence,
For I know your decision to go was one made in fury.
Unaware of your choices,
The lingering voices which fill your head,
Are not mine. They are your own.
Telling yourself you were wrong.
You could never listen, you could never admit defeat.
Always victorious, you laugh at my rules, my narrow path.
If only now you could see - you have been defeated.
Damocles' sword hangs over you,
But I am holding it firmly and I will never let go.
With my other hand I reach out to you.
I will always wait, eager for the day when you return to me,
Welcoming my embrace, instead of profaning the hand that reared you.
I will never lose hope, for
I know what it is to be tempted.

Rachel Parris (15)
Loughborough High School

HOPE

A cold, crisp autumn morning.
I woke at the wake of dawn.
They had been up for hours,
Now I could hear the tone in their voices start to
Sadden.

I had been dreading the approach of this morning,
The morning I knew I would never
Forget.

Now it faced me square on, like a brick wall,
The only way was over.

I went downstairs as he gathered his bags together,
He looked up and smiled gently just as the harsh rap at the door
invaded our
Warm
Loving home.

Two large men stood before us,
Solemnly.

He turned to us, tears twinkling in his warm but
Sad eyes.
He embraced us all for the last time,
We didn't know when the next time would be.
Then he was
Gone.

The big, black car drove him away,
Silently.
If we'd ever see him again
We didn't know.
All we had was
Hope.

Gemma Mahon (16)
The Rutland College

A Victim Of Love

The bruised face.
The swollen lips. They tell their own story.
I remember her now.
Crouched in the corner. Whimpering like a child.

And him.
His fists beating her beautiful face.
Cruel flesh smashing against fragile skin.
Breaking the delicate bones beneath.

Salty tears mingle with warm, sticky blood.
My own tears trace a path over my pale face.
I gaze at the whimpering, wounded creature.
My mother.

Nothing more than a mass of blood and broken bones.
I cannot stop him.
My plaster-encased arm warns me what will happen if I try.
His torture continues still.

Her cries of pain sear my brain.
Frustrations boils my blood.
I watch them silently.
Pain-filled screams assaulting my tiny ears.

I do not hear them.

And after.
When blood is wiped clean.
Broken bones are mended.
Tempers soothed and rage spent.

I ask her why.
Her beautiful, broken face turns to me.
Simply, she says

I love him.

Leonie Ross (16)
The Rutland College

CONTEMPLATION

I climb
climb to the top of the building
I feel surprisingly calm and at peace.
However, then I reach the edge
Look down a thousand feet to the road
The black cabs now as small as ants
And the buses the size of ladybirds
Tiny pinhead people get on with their lives
All carefree and happy
To them this dusty city is home
For me it is an impersonal hell
Full of people who do not speak
Just glance over the top of their newspapers.
Why did he do this to me?
The one person I trusted
And devoted my life to
Desolate
St. Paul's - large in the mist
My hands feel sticky
Sweaty palms, racing heart
Loneliness
And before I go
I think of him.

Rachel Lowe (16)
The Rutland College

TONIGHT

Walking back yesterday avoiding involvement
I stumbled across a frozen soul white as fear
As I approached, it scrambled away revealing scars from the
claws of death
It moved as it could which was not much
This crippled, terrified tiny soul sparked within me pity, sorrow
And morbid guilt for I knew only too well the owner and past
victims of those claws
A split decision, I make my choice
To let it freeze and die, or offer an angel-like hand

Cradled within my fists, frenzy takes over
It is fear, the aftershock, the sense of danger
So trying not to further injure those fragile wings
An irony arises, the protection it gains, is the very box that
carries those claws
Perhaps sensing this murderous presence
It is still once again, unmoving, silent, blank-eyed, but all of
one emotion: fear

I ponder my decision, present water, nuts
Then I have done all I can, and say 'It's up to you'
And as I cover the light, I wonder how it must be,
In the dark. Alone. Not knowing life from death.

A new morning in my life at least, now I shall see if there is
another besides
Ravenous for all I have to offer, a mix of fear but inquisitive
It explores all it can see, paranoia yet joy, moving with relief,
it is not the only one
But as I release my night-long breath I am faced with another choice
It dawns upon me with a sigh and some sorrow
What will I do? Let this little soul go, is it strong enough or
permanently crippled

Shall I turn it over like a corpse to the Authorities
Best not to decide, is that the right choice?
Give today then maybe this night
I will turn the choice over to the other, let it decide

And it's choice?
I do not know for today is today and tonight's decision
has not yet come.

Neville Collins (16)
The Rutland College

ONE DAY

I'll tidy my bedroom.
And walk to save car fumes.
One day.

I'll ring my old friend.
And help put child abuse to an end.
One day.

I'll clean that dusty shelf.
And fund raise for fatal health.
One day.

I'll sort out those old books.
And make sure everyone gave more than they took.
One day.

One day might be too late.
Not everybody has time to wait.

Julie Elizabeth Russell (16)
The Rutland College

LOST WITHIN THE CAVERNS OF THE MIND

The flickering illumination highlights the way ahead.

Only down

The way behind is blocked, and the only path leads onwards

And downwards

The circle is closing, there seems to be no way out, only
onwards and downwards
Onwards and downwards, to the unmentionable terror at the bottom,
a place of no return.
The spiral must be broken, the crushing vice escaped.
You look around at the passage that you are in:
A million memories, a trove of gems is picked up, admired, and
placed back

Down again.

You cannot buy your freedom, not even with such riches as these.

Alone with the flickering light held aloft, you look back.
The gentle slope upwards is blocked - completely impassable,
and the road ahead is only going

Down, steeper and steeper, like a helter-skelter to hell.
Frantically you look around:
Is there no way to escape from this bitter trap?

You run
Faster and faster, your solitary light flashing on the stone walls
of the cavern.

Faster and faster and faster

Down and down and down

Until you suddenly collapse,

Lost within the caverns of the mind.

Ben Tassell (16)
The Rutland College

EMPTINESS

Drained of all emotions,
Lying crumpled on the kitchen floor,
Just last week I felt so proud,
Until I heard the news.

Only a week ago today,
He'd left me for his country.
Then you came by yesterday,
With a telegram in your hand.

He's gone you said, to somewhere good,
Where birds will always sing.
And where angels can take care of him,
And where flowers always bloom.

The last words I heard him say,
Are ones I'll never forget.
'Don't worry Mum, I'll be back soon.'
Now all his plans are shattered.

I can still see him in my mind,
I felt so very proud.
Now I sit here all alone,
My worst nightmares have come true.

Kathryn Sanders (16)
The Rutland College

LETTER FROM A SOLDIER

Struggles all round but I'm fighting empty air
Complaining about battles that simply aren't there
Oh why do we moan about the little things around us
Aspire to leave our easy peace with wings which 'free' us
And fly to enjoy life's better things that will always tease us
Come on and rescue me.

Endure the battlefield of lies and hate
Watch out my bait, oh no! Too late!
Battle for love, a soul mate to share the lust
Learn to kill whom you cannot trust
Learn to survive when dreams turn to dust
Learn to defend, counter, parry, thrust!
Come on and free me.

It's a letter from a soldier
A cry of help from an innocent man
Please come and rescue me
Wash this blood clean off my hands.

Soldier on leave from a day of duty
Relaxing in the home, spreading flowers so purely
Screwing on the silencer, guerrilla warfare
Defence never dropped for a second but attack doesn't care
Family slaughtered and slashed, murder everywhere, loyalty laid bare
Why won't you rescue me?
Come back! Please rescue me
The gun behind my back is for protection you see.

It's a letter from a soldier
A plea from a lonely man
Fighting battles in his head, soon we'll all be dead
Nothing will wash the blood clean off my hands.

Please come and rescue me
Yours truly,
A soldier.

Michael Record (16)
The Rutland College

INSECURITY

The tears dried and the skin became tight,
She had not expected this raging fight,
He accused her and she accused him,
But it was unproductive and time-consuming.

A sarcastic laugh came out of her mouth,
Their destinies seemingly one north and one south,
But she was naive and chose to ignore it,
how could he still pretend, or she misinterpret?

Racing thoughts and clammy hands,
This has shattered their future plans.

But as dawn breaks, lightening the room
And the radio-alarm plays its tune,
She opens her eyes and looks to her side,
She sees the man who apparently lied.

A deep breath and a sigh of relief,
Awakening erases her pain and grief.

Michelle Lee (16)
The Rutland College

HOMESICK CHILD

I wake to the sound of alarm clocks,
Only to realise that it's reality ringing.
I wake to loneliness, fear and independence.

'Showers are free!' are the next words I hear.
Shame it's not the voice that I'm used to hearing.
It's a stranger, someone I've known for two weeks.
I slowly get out of bed hoping that if I close
My eyes I'll be back home,
With my family.
Only to realise that when I open them,
I'm still in the same dark room.

I stumble across clothes and bags.
Reaching for my towel, I pull open the door
And slowly leave the room.
I'm in a daze; the shower walk is a routine.
It's all a routine.
I stand under the hot shower, remembering how
The sun used to hit me.
The steamed room allows me to dream once again.

I'm interrupted.
Someone's walked in.
I grab the soap and smother myself in bubbles.
Then it's the shampoo and conditioner.
I step out of my little paradise to a
Freezing cold floor and an icy cold breeze hits
My face.

I want to jump back to where I was,
But it's gone now.
Gone until the next morning,
Where I can dream again.

I walk down the hall and back to my room,
Where everything is different.
I stand there;
Vulnerability is wrapping herself around me.
I can't escape.
I dread tomorrow.
Will I be able to withstand it for yet another day?
Will I stay sane?

Rana Darwish (16)
The Rutland College

365 DAYS

The beginning, full of hope.
It's familiar but new, year awaits me.

The winding road, the blanket of snow,
Melted and revealed . . .
The trail of skis
And the crosses behind.
The tears and pain,
Will scar me forever.

The months of waiting passed by
And revealed . . .
The distress of exams
And sighs of dismay.
The overwhelmed faces
Will live with me forever.

The beginning, full of hope.
It's familiar but new, year awaits me.

Rebecca Allison
The Rutland College

NOT SURE

I have been given the task of writing a poem,
I don't know where to start or even where it's going.

But when writing a poem,
Where do you start
It seems to me to be an art.

When some people start they just can't stop,
But once they have finished,
I'm still stuck at the top.

The first step in writing is to think of a subject,
Some people can think of many,
at the moment I can't think of any.

Once I have started I usually stop,
go back to the beginning
and restart from the top.

I have no hope when writing a poem
I don't know where it will start
Let alone where it's going.

In a poem you can use,
Stanzas, similes with punctuation,
metaphors, rhyme and alliteration.
Use either, neither or all you can choose.

But the most important thing is inspiration,
Whether fate, love, life, people or alienation.
When you write the poem you could write it for someone.
Whether your brother, sister, aunt, uncle, dad or mum.

So once you have your inspiration,
Pick up a pen and begin your creation.
Don't stop, keep on going,
and in the end you'll have your own poem.

Laura Girvan (16)
The Rutland College

THE ONLY WAY TO FIND THE ANSWERS IS TO EXPERIENCE THE QUESTION

So why is it that . . .

The passion of hate
Confuses the desire to love?
The distance between two people
Forms emptiness inside?
The touch of a beloved
Stabilises the feeling of security?
The frustration of rejection
Mirrors the satisfaction of achievement?
The greed of attention
Highlights the feeling of paranoia?
The selfishness of suicide
Explains the lonesome person?
The fear of death
Shadows the reason to live happily?

Emotions form a circle
Even though we live on a line.
Never knowing when it's going to end or better still
Why?

Victoria Simmons (16)
The Rutland College

THE TREE

Tall and stately, arms outstretched,
waiting for the spring to come,
First the buds and then the leaves,
and then the blossom in the breeze.

Towering in the forest glade,
putting everything in the shade,
with leaves of multi-colours,
looking more attractive than the others.

In the autumn the leaves are falling,
and the tree is bare and brown,
children play in the leaves,
throwing them all around.

The tree sleeps on in the winter,
thinking about the spring when it arrives.
Oh, what a joy it is,
to have a new lease of life.

Elizabeth Gomersall (17)
The Rutland College

THE TREE

The trunk looks scaly like a dragon's body.
The body of the tree had flaking skin.
At the bottom of the tree it looks like an opening
to a dark cave.
The tree looks like a long winding path.
The top view reminded me of an island.

James Docker (16)
The Rutland College

IT ALL DEPENDS

It was really very difficult
Deciding what to write.
Lots of thoughts were in my mind,
But no poem was in sight.

Then at once it dawned on me,
The idea was so clear.
A very special person,
Was sat so very near.

His name I cannot tell you,
That's for my own protection.
For if I did, I fear that I'd
Be a victim of rejection.

One day I will tell him
What my feelings are,
But I have a feeling
I won't get very far.

There is no body language,
No looks or smiles returned,
In which case you can surely say
My efforts have been spurned.

Maybe he's just very shy,
Or totally unaware,
I haven't been that obvious,
I never sit and stare.

So maybe we'll end up together,
Or maybe just be friends.
I know for sure my thoughts on him,
So on him it all depends.

Sarah Langdon (17)
The Rutland College

TRAPPED

I'm sorry if I cut you off
And hide inside my own mind
But I'm so used to coping by myself
It's hard to let you in

For years my problems have been my own
The bottle just keeps filling
So long its all been trapped inside
How long before it shatters?

I really want to let you in
I wish I'd let you help me
But open up, allow you in
I think that that might break me

But I don't want to burden you
With problems which are my own
You already have a lot to deal with
What use would adding to it be?

Yet I wish that you could read me
Tell what's going on inside
Know, when I escape into my mind
That it's not you I pull away from

So don't let me cut you off
Make me answer all your questions
And if I seem to drift away from you
Please push and you will save me.

Amy Meehan (16)
The Rutland College

REALITY

Green was the grass,
Blue the sky,
I skipped past some friendly passers-by.
Bees buzzed,
And birds went tweet,
Sweet now bitter,
Bitter now sweet,
Sad now happy,
Rain now sun,
Everyone upon this wonderful planet is having fun.

Then I woke -
Muddy still the grass,
Grey still the sky,
I nervously shuffle past
Some weary passers-by,
Roads still clogged with traffic,
The air still blocked with smog,
Mothers at only twelve,
Still afraid of next-door's dog,
Drug pushers and alcoholics,
Marijuana, Crack and E,
Aerosols, needles and solvents,
This is reality.

Jessica Emberton (16)
The Rutland College

AN EMOTIONAL PLEA

I can play the fool
But I feel no humour.
I can understand
But am not understood.
I can be in love
And feel no emotion.

I can be scared
But am not afraid.
I can listen
But keep my ears shut.
I can see
And yet be blind.

I can teach
But not be taught.
I can be an individual
But stand in a crowd.
I can scream
          And yet be silent.

Emily Ryder (16)
The Rutland College

VOICE WITHIN A CHILD

People can be so cruel without even realising,
Leave some people crying and some people shining,
Some are left hurt and others will sigh,
Don't worry about me, I'll get by.

Why don't they care; they're doing so well,
They can live on, be it a boy or a girl,
Deep in the blue, purple and green,
True thoughts are inside, they cannot be seen.

The world flashes by and nobody stops
Yes! They can see, but no they cannot.
Everyone's blind to what they know,
It's like the whole world's silent as in rain or snow.

Come what may and they say it will come,
What's done is done so please don't be glum,
For your life's planned out before you
There's no changing that,
No way of knowing and you can't turn back.

Hannah Clarke (16)
The Rutland College

DO YOU REMEMBER?

I stand here today
and I see through the tears.
A reflection of the years.

I remember

the first dizzy spell,
the days of truth,
the countless lunch times,
the glitter evening.

I remember

the caring questions,
the guiding hand,
the inspiration, admiration
and the drive.

I remember . . .

do you?

Samantha Baxter (16)
The Rutland College

LIFE

Boredom, although information,
Physical, without sensation.
T
  r
    a
      i
       l
         s of hopeless

individuals

walking through their mechanical lives.
Freedom in chains,
happiness in vain.

Talking without words,
Communications not heard,
Modern life   *Modern death.*
Fickle minds of admiration,
a life we live of adoration
for ourselves . . .

. . . and only us.

Heidi Marshall (16)
The Rutland College

LOVERS

Please believe me when I say
It wasn't meant to be this way.
I was meant to be with you,
We'd stick together through and through.
But not everything that's meant to be
works out the way it's s'posed to be,
and please believe me when I say
it wasn't meant to be this way.

And now we're here, just like before.
Your smiling face as you walk through the door.
And I feel now as I felt back then,
but I can't take you back again.
So forgive me dear if I make you cry,
and I'll wipe these tears from my own eyes.
I know your hurt won't last forever,
just until you find another lover.

Rachael Webster (16)
The Rutland College

SKI '99

Great expectations were
soon shattered along with our eardrums as we
were subjected to the fourth playing of M People's song,

'Moving on up.'

The simple shell of the shack
was protected by the posture of
the mountains,

moving on up

towards the sky the lifts took us,
the spray from our boots
a common occurrence as we continued

moving on up

in ability.
We were classed as three star,
skiers lined the hospital corridors,
great expectations were shattered here too -
two twisted knees.

Julie Fursdon (16)
The Rutland College

THE UNKNOWN

The door is open, and the darkness shines through.
It slithers by my side and against my feet,
It ends at the steps below me.
As I begin to walk, my sight is blurred,
My feet are heavy and my head is light.
I turn to find the door closed and darkness surrounds me.

As I begin to walk, my steps are small and shallow.
I can see a flicker of light in front
And as I walk further, the light becomes brighter,
The air becomes warmer and my heart beats with all its might.
As images of fright flash before me, I pray that the outside
will hear my cries.

Though this place, that began to haunt me
Is now beginning to fill me with calmness
And what I assumed was a place of fear, is in fact a place of desire.

Sophie Broadwell (16)
The Rutland College

LONELY

You're part of a group but you do not fit in,
Whenever you speak you feel it's a sin.
They talk about what they did last weekend,
And about the new top they are planning to lend.

Whenever you phone there's nobody in,
But you know that tomorrow you'll hear where they've been.
The jokes and the smiles all exclude you,
You wish you could move and start something new.

They try to be nice and laugh at your jokes,
But they cringe whenever you don't mention blokes.
You wish that you didn't really care,
But you know they'd not notice if you weren't even there.

You're happy when it's the end of the day,
And you can leave and just get away.
You rush to get somewhere that feels warm and homely,
Because the rest of the time you feel so lonely.

Sarah Basden (16)
The Rutland College

TOGETHER AT LAST

Laughing, smiling, staring,
across the crowded room.
Feelings growing between the two, unknown.

The spell was broken,
unleashed from inside.
Two hearts joined as one.

Both had felt loneliness,
Unhappiness, insecurity.
Heartache.

Together, they experienced new and different things,
to touch, to see,
as they'd never before.

Together,
they had now become whole.

Kim Mellor (16)
The Rutland College

THE SOLUTION

How do you mend a broken heart?
A piece of sellotape should do the trick
or maybe a jagged smear of prittstick
none of these seem to mend my broken heart
How do I stop my eyes from crying?
Keeping them shut might prevent the tears
but I can't go on like that for another two years
How do I stop the sad songs from playing?
Push my fingers tightly into both ears
finding myself no longer susceptible to hearing
my worst fears
there's the solution, I'll just keep my fingers
tightly in both ears.

Gemma Wheatley (16)
The Rutland College

THE TREE

The long winding tree bends on a water slide,
unwrapping.
It is rough, bumpy, and I imagine strong, it looks
like an Octopus Island.
The tree looks like a joining of a new life, but a
disgusting one.
It's a cliff on that waterside, unwrapping like flaking
dead skin.
The tree is an abstract green disease, on a long
winding path.
It's a sad person, dark at its depth.

Emily Boden (16)
The Rutland College

FOREVER

I am here and you are not
You've gone again, I must have forgot
Now I sit all alone
The room around me feeling like stone
I drift away to some place hotter
And what could be better
As you were there?
I make every moment with you last
Until I realise it was all in the past
Reality hits you like a thousand knives
And all anyone can hear are my cries.
I long to see you one last time
And in my heart of hearts
Hope that you will be mine . . .
Forever.

Sarah Marsh (16)
The Rutland College

THE TREE

The tree is a cliff on an island,
Revealing a sad person
Standing in the opening of a dark cave
With an octopus with a green disease.

It is a water slide going
Into the opening of the dark cave.

It is an abstract sculpture of
The world's continents slotting together.

The tree looks like a swirl of flaking skin.

Lucy Murton (16)
The Rutland College

THE LONER

She sits.
To the untrained eye, a woman with no direction,
approaching the conclusion of a futile existence.

She thinks.
To me she is deep in thought.
Her mind whirring, like a contortionist in a treasure chest,
bursting with ideas awaiting release, but that
no one can or cares to hear.
But me.

She closes her eyes.
Comforted by the certainty of her own mortality.
She realises that the difference between open and shut
is no more than a difference in darkness . . .
She sleeps.

Kerry Bowers (16)
The Rutland College

THE TREE

The tree reminds me of a disease;
It is green and quiet and abstract.
The tree is a fish with scaly skin:
It looks as though it's dying.

It also is a person with flaky skin.
It is sad and lonely as it lies like broccoli,
But at the same time
It's big and fierce like a dragon.

It is a cave opening with a long swirl path.

Deborah Gough (17)
The Rutland College

RAW TALENT

Runs like the wind between the trees.
Losing defenders in a whirlwind of speed and brilliance.
Only he can perform such acrobatics, such amazing skill.
No one can hope to emulate the master.
Many have tried but none have even come close.

Alone in this world his brilliance shines out,
Dazzling all with his sweeping talents.
Love is so easy for him, with his talent and
Worldly magic exhibited before all.
Dances through the field of play, like a leaping gazelle,
Chasing through all obstructions.
Over and under players, in and out, then he strikes, like a scorpion,
Sending the ball into the back of the net.

The crowd roars 'Ronaldo.'

Anthony Vernon (16)
The Rutland College

THE TREE

The tree looks like it freely grows arms,
Sprouting out like a head of broccoli
And moves freely in the wind.

With the bends of the tree
Is the joining of new life
Like a never-ending path
Swirling from beneath.
As the bark flakes off,
It is a snake shedding its skin.

Dee Cowling (16)
The Rutland College

THE TREE

The tree is a long winding path connecting
And unwrapping a sad person's pet octopus
which has a green disease.

The tree is an octopus standing on a long winding path
Holding a piece of broccoli and some ice-cream
Whilst creating an abstract sculpture.

The tree reminds me of a scaly-like dragon
standing in the opening of a dark cave.

The tree reminds of a cliff
Unwrapping a green disease of flaking skin
to reveal a dead person.

The tree reminds me of an island on the world's continents
Slotting together to reveal a new life.

Dee Martin (16)
The Rutland College

THE TREE

The tree looks like the world where all the continents slot together.
But it falls apart like skin of a dead person.
Some of the branches look like a road map twisting and turning to
lead you to the city.
At the base it looks and reminds people of dark caves because of the
formation of the shadows.

Jordan Crawford (17)
The Rutland College

FORGIVENESS

Whatever you did and whatever you do
I forgive you.
Whatever you saw and whatever you see
I forgive you.

No matter what you do
You can turn darkness to light.
You work miracles on those around you
Throughout the day and night.

Wherever you are and wherever you've been
I forgive you.
Whatever you saw and whatever you've seen
I forgive you.

No matter how you look
You can always light the way.
Nobody can ever discourage you
Or ever dampen your day.

I forgive you
No matter what.
I forgive you
No matter what.
I forgive you.

Lucy Grey (16)
The Rutland College

NICE TO LOOK AT

Get some pretty people,
cover them in plastic,
scoop out their insides,
and sell them until they drop dead.
And then prop them up.

Looking deep and meaningful,
spilling someone else's guts,
spilling someone else's guts.
Once, somewhere, and to someone,
it probably meant something.

Empty shells with pretty smiles, to some it appeals.
They admire, aspire to be, and worship these pretty smiles.
Nice to look at, maybe beautiful to some,

But not real.
Real is not pretty or beautiful, real has bits missing, real has scars.
Real people are a messy pattern of imperfections,
that's how you recognise them.

And now, face value is being sold as emotional Pollyfilla.
Switch on the TV,
Say hello to the emotional prostitutes.

Sam Carter (16)
The Rutland College

NOT TODAY

The repeated sight of black and white stripes
Like a zebra running from a predator
But we won't be running
Not today.

The huge roars of humanity
Like a lion battling with an enemy
But we won't be defeated by our enemy,
Not today.

The cluster of people moving back and forth,
Like an army of ants following one another,
But we won't follow the unsuccessful,
Not today.

The dismal look of the opposition
Like a cat's expression when being chased,
But we won't be chased from our goal,
Not today.

The memory of that game,
The sight,
The sound
And all from just our football ground.

Louise Allison (16)
The Rutland College

A PASSION FOR FASHION

My passion is fashion,
Style is my religion,
My god is the designer not the supreme being,
However my faith is often misinterpreted,
Vanity.

I have no shame,
No shame frees me,
Frees me from the chains of conformity,
Frees me to express myself as an individual.

I despise lack of thought, lack of imagination,
Fashion today is more than clothes,
Fashion is your lifestyle,
To sort out your life, you must sort out your style.

Without individuality, the world would be a dull place,
A place where everyone was an animal, a sheep aimlessly
                                        following the flock,
What is the point in being like everyone else?

A life without fashion and style is a life with one interest,
                                        interest in fitting in,
Why does everyone feel a need to fit in?
Why does it take years of inner turmoil, of wanting to belong,
                        to make people realise to fit in is boring?
Real joy in life is to stand out,
To be proud of who you are.

James Robinson (17)
The Rutland College

A PASSION FOR FOOTBALL

Football,
In my veins,
In my blood,
In my mind,
In my heart,
When match day comes,
There's a silent hush,
Nerves and all, adrenaline rush.

Half-past two,
Fans start to queue,
Ground is filling,
Overspilling,
A sea of red is all I see,
It signifies our loyalty.

Impatient feet take up their places,
Anticipation on all their faces.
Smells fill the air and make me choke,
Burgers, pies, tobacco smoke.

Then the ground erupts,
When out on the pitch
Come the eleven men that I
Worship.

Paul Richardson (16)
The Rutland College

PICTURE IMPERFECT

Beyond the superficial illusion
That hides a thousand situations
I see her, for what she is.
Sparkled, sapphire eyes once hung on a backdrop of white
Are now dissolved into a sea of yellow,
Tainted red eyes.

Ebony mane falls past her shoulders, straight as arrows,
Sprinkled with middle age and worry,
Cropped and waved. Split ends rule.

Beautiful skin,
Reflecting the light but shining in her own.
Thereafter lined by the hardship she endures.

A smile creeps up the sides of her face.
Blood red lips. Bursting to the brim with newness,
Reduced now to pale emptiness.

Gladly she lays down her wants,
leaving her youth behind
And receiving nothing in return.

My mother, the hero.

Lucy Crowley (16)
The Rutland College

OPEN DAY

Empty eyes, and vacant faces,
All the friends take their places,
My eyes search for the back-row spaces,
Met by people's cold, blank gazes.

Is this right? Do I look the same?
Endless panic in my brain.
I feel my strength begin to fade,
As I look up, to see I'm last again.

Haze of people, spinning round,
Mass of voices; a deafening sound.
As I reach the door, I turn around
And the tears are falling on the ground.

I can do this, it's for me,
It doesn't matter that I 'can't see'.
This is where I want to be,
Another try at being free.

Another hour, and it's the end,
But then a voice, and the tears mend.
I found a place, where I don't pretend,
The end of the day, and I found a friend.

Ruth Tolkien (16)
The Rutland College

A DISTANT NIGHTMARE THAT WILL NEVER LIE DORMANT

If only the ambulance had got to him in time,
If only his life wasn't laid on the line,
If only he didn't leave so soon,
He would have seen that his life was destined to bloom.

If only they weren't driving so fast,
If only the latest threat wasn't the last,
If only I'd forced him to come clean,
Then this tragedy would never have been.

That seemed to be the worst day ever,
Until the coffin came,
To say goodbye for one last time,
I've never felt so much to blame.

He asked for help!
He cried for help!
He pleaded . . .
. . . But I didn't know how to help!

They ended a life,
It is clear to see,
They have blood on their hands,
Murderers they will always be.

One day they might realise
That those tears I had in my eyes,
Will be there forever.

Sophie Zielinka (17)
The Rutland College

IMAGINE YOUR LIFE AS A ROSE

Imagine your life as a rose
    - grown from a seed,
        growing upwards as far as it can,
Avoiding all the weeds.
Being trained and twined along its path,
        being made to look its best,
           sprouting leaves and thorns all over,
Like hairy legs and chest.

Eventually it buds
    - the beginning of its bloom,
        still tightly encased until it splits -
It'll unravel very soon.
One by one its petals unfold
    - new events occur with each,
It opens and relaxes,
And for a time it's a beauty - the best it'll ever be!
Vibrant and voluptuous, a sight you'll want to see.

Unfortunately next its downfall begins,
    - its petals darken and dry,
        they loosen and fall from the once ripe bud,
- The rose has begun to die.

When all the petals are gone for good,
        and its seeds dispersed from its centre,
        - its reason for living has been fulfilled -
           its daughter will grow this winter.

Annabel Pettigrew (16)
The Rutland College

EMOTIONS

It starts like a dream,
A dream I didn't want to lose.
The warmth, the engraving emotions
The obsessive avidity
Empathy.
Feelings imprisoned so deep,
These irrational emotions I clasp
- Unable to let go.

This apathetic world in which we live,
With all its traitors and conspiracies,
So apparently callous.
Yet I turn a heedless eye
- Absorbed by distracting thoughts.

I'm still searching -
Helplessly searching for an explanation.
Why can no one release me?
That lost key to opening my heart
Lies in the hand of another soul,
The hand of the person I desire
No one can release me from these emotions
- But He.

Abbey-Gail Goddard (17)
The Rutland College

FRIENDSHIP

When the world feels like it's ending
And you see no way to get through
When you're feeling all alone
Like no one's there for you.

It's always the same people
That make you smile again
That reminds you of your good points
And take away your pain.

When your problems feel larger than life
And you want to end it all
When you feel your living in a black hole
Who do you always call?

When you think of the mistakes you've made
And you want to run and hide
It's your mates you'll always turn to
Because they'll stand by your side.

So next time you're feeling all alone
Make sure you look around
They're never very far away
There's always a friend to be found.

Amy Whiteoak (16)
The Rutland College

DID YOU EVER . . .

Did you ever really love me,
like I loved you?
When you said it did you mean it?
How I wish your love was true.

Did you ever really need me,
like I needed you?
To hug and to hold me,
when I was sad and blue.

Did you ever really want me,
like I wanted you?
Or was it just all total lies,
lies all the way through?

Did you ever really trust me,
like I trusted you?
But I shouldn't have should I?
as you messed that up too.

Did you ever really love me,
like I loved you?
It really was love you know;
how I wish you loved me too!

Lucy Gandy (16)
The Rutland College

DRUGS

Drugs are fireworks
They make you high
You shoot higher and higher
The more you buy.

Drugs are Catherine wheels
Spinning you around
You just can't stop
Until you run out.

Once you have seen it
You want more and more
Your life revolves around
Making a score.

Drugs are bangers
They blow your mind
You're lying on the floor
Wasted and blind.

In the end drugs are fireworks
They make you high
But at what cost
Do you reach the sky?

Craig Wilson (13)
Uppingham Community College

A RATHER STRANGE AND SLITHERY TEACHER

The teacher slithered into the screeching class,
'Ssssssh' he hissed.
'SsssssSam sssstop that you naughty boy
come to my basket after the lesson.
Now classss, today we're going to study
Sssssssience.'
The teacher slithered around handing out exercise books
'Now get on with your work quickly.'
Halfway through the lesson
A screwed up paper ball flew across the room towards the teacher,
It hit with deadly aim.
The teacher quickly turned his head to its source,
he transfixed the child with his hypnotising eyes.
The room is now like a morgue.

Russell Kent-Payne (12)
Uppingham Community College

MY DOG BRUNO

My dog Bruno comes out of his kennel.
He roars.
His sharp eye spots a cat
On his quick paws
He flies down the garden
He thinks he's got a chance this time.
He's right behind the big black cat
He jumps into the air
But the cat's no longer there.
He was just too late again
But I know he'll try next time.

Ian Young (12)
Uppingham Community College

THE MOLE

We enter the classroom, he's there as usual - digging around
in a box full of papers.
His glasses slip down his nose, revealing small squinting
eyes. Then he starts wittering, mumbling to himself in French.
'Bonjour tout le monde'
'Bonjour Monsieur' echoes the uninterested students.
He proceeds with the lesson, but then, a boy at the back
mutters something to his neighbours.
He looks at the boy over his glasses with cold eyes piercing
him like a knife.
'Would you care to repeat that young man?' He questions.
'Nnnnno Sir' the boy stammers.
'Well let's go on with the lesson then.'
The then silent class groan and sigh with the thought
of another boring French lesson.

Charlotte Driver (12)
Uppingham Community College

FOOTBALL

Football is life, a game of two halves.
You can win or lose but you can't have a snooze.
You start with a kick off, you haven't a choice,
100 per cent you must give, you play the game and do your best.
You can do things right and you can do things wrong,
But half time doesn't take all that long.
In the next half you get more tired.
If you've worked really hard you'll feel like a rest.
But you carry on working and keep doing your best,
When the game's over the whistle will blow
And you'll be finished and ready to go.

Sean Beeby (13)
Uppingham Community College

MOON

The moon, it's a wonderful place,
The moon, it looks like a face,
The moon, it's made of cheese,
If you look at it too long, it'll make you sneeze.

The moon, it's in the shape of a ball,
Its light reflects down the hall,
The moon, it's large and round,
The moon, it was lost then found.

But when the moon is full,
You have to be very careful,
There are strange creatures about
And you might get caught out.

Sam Fletcher (13)
Uppingham Community College

MILLENNIUM EVE

Just imagine the excitement, the fun,
Everybody happy, every single one.
Things have happened this year,
Last year and before,
Everything will go down in history.
Including the hatred and the war.
The bad things should be put to a stop,
War, poverty, the lot.

A lot of things this century have been great,
But remember,
All of these things have been decided, by the
Future voice of fate.

Bethany Perrin (12)
Uppingham Community College

THE SEA HORSE

The sea is a wild horse
White and free,
She has no one to tame her,
Her spirit of glee.
Day after day she gallops,
Her mane untidy and loose.
Her hooves, the stones.
As she places them on the shore.
Her head,
Her large exciting eyes,
Is the top of the wave,
She enjoys every moment.
She is a wave,
Like over a jump,
Up, up and up.
High into the air
And down she goes.

Elizabeth Blockley (13)
Uppingham Community College

LAUGHTER IS LIKE AN ERUPTING VOLCANO

Laughter is like an erupting volcano,
It explodes from time to time,
Never knowing the real reason why,
Lava flows like laughter,
While heated with joy.
It spits out loud thundering noises,
The lava slowly starts setting,
Whilst the laughter starts quietening.

Emily Stillman (13)
Uppingham Community College

FORESTS ARE FOREVER

Forests are forever
Leaves a rustling, leaves a rustling
Whisper, whisper the trees will say the secrets of the wind
Around the trees, the wind will whirl, the birds will
glide with utmost lift.
Suddenly the birds break the silence with a boost of triumph.
The rain starts cascading through the canopy
Raindrops plunged through the leaves drenching the ground below
The birds forget their cheerful song and fly away to dryer places.
The forest becomes silent again and all you can hear is the
drip, drip, drop
The leopardess runs with her cubs afollowing, dodging
boughs and vines
The dormouse snuffles among the now sodden leaves
The panther following the unaware boar ready to pounce
for a teatime gnaw.
The leaves on the large pines rustling in the evening breeze.
The darkness draws near, the birds fly to their beds for the night
As the gloom and dusk descends from the tree tops
The forest falls into a deep . . . dark . . . slumber . . . sleep.

Vicki Parkin (13)
Uppingham Community College

SILENCE

The world is a deadly silence,
All creatures dead and silent.
Coldness is in the air,
It is still and I am lonely.

Can no one hear my cry?
Here where I lie, I dream of why,
The war had begun,
There down the lane.

I hear a cry of pain,
Can I make it
Or am I too late?
There by the gate lies the body,
I must continue my hard journey.

I see the house darker than ever,
Someone must be there,
Where I hear no laughter,
Surely my family is still there.

Anneka Howard (12)
Uppingham Community College

THE RIVER

Life is like a river, flowing down every crevice, trying to find a
reason for everything.
At first the tiny spring, starting its journey into the big wide
world.

Slowly picking up speed, crashing into cracks and creeping up
crevices, like a toddler beginning to walk, examining every path,
trying to find a way out.

As the river matures, it calms down and flows into the age of
the student, not bothering to examine unknown crevices,
preferring to go along with the steady pace of life.

Then comes the age of the calm meandering middle age. Flowing
along with the grace of a king. Slowly caressing stones from
the rough bedrock, like a mother stroking the hair of her child.

Lastly comes the age of the old frail river, spreading out into
the big wide sea, like a blanket covering the ocean, the river is
gone, but soon a new river will flow.

Tom Bysouth (13)
Uppingham Community College

THE FOREST WALK

Prowling through the forest
Softly padding
Peering through the darkness
Searching for movement.

There, under that bush
A scurry of tiny paws
A small object scuttles across my path
Oh no, I missed!

Admiring the forest scenery
With tall trees and thick bushes
With vines and leaves
And the old, winding, peaceful stream.

The howl of a monkey
The squawk of a parrot
The hissing, rustling of a snake
Just add more to the forest atmosphere.

The soft smell of pine
The rich smell of wet leaves
The scent of dew on the ground
Wait, the scent of a mouse!

Prowling through the forest
Softly padding
Peering through the darkness
Searching for the movement of a tiger's prey.

Andrew Bryant (13)
Uppingham Community College

FUTURE WORLD

What will the world be like
For children everywhere
When the new millennium dawns
Who will be there to care?

What will the world be like
For animals big and small
When food becomes more scarce
Who for help will call?

What will the world be like
When I become a mum
With children of my own
From where will all help come?

What will the world be like
When my children are all grown
And living their new lives
What will they call home?

What will the world be like
Tomorrow when I wake
I'm sure it'll be the same
Life's fun for goodness sake!

Carys Armstrong (13)
Uppingham Community College

ARMAGEDDON

The last weapon has been fired,
The last wounded man is dead,
The political voices are silenced
And the last death threat has been said,
No more feelings to be felt,
No more tears are to be shed,
All of this has happened,
Because the last human being is dead,
No more Christmas parties,
No more childhood dreams
And no longer on the battlefield,
Will you hear a single scream.
Some books will never be written,
Some books will never be read,
None of this will happen,
Because the last man on Earth is dead.

Mathew Waik (12)
Uppingham Community College

CLOUDS

The clouds are full of pictures
Of anything you want them to be.
From a dragon breathing fire
To anything you desire.
We turn another corner to see
A kangaroo, then a gush of wind
Splits the clouds in two.

Jemma Higley (13)
Uppingham Community College

IMAGINE

Imagine.
The earth floating in total emptiness,
Left torn after all the hate,
The wars and endless destruction.
The nuclear bombs have turned the grass a funny colour,
The oceans are no longer blue,
But black.
In its last moments all the volcanoes erupt,
Lava and toxic fumes spewing out everywhere,
You wouldn't recognise it,
There are no screams of survivors.
There is no one left.
But you . . .
Silence.
The world is dead.

Rupert Jenkyn-Jones (12)
Uppingham Community College

THE RAINFOREST

The rainforest is like an apple,
It's ready to be eaten up,
Green with colour, shining in the light,
Red when humans are ready to bite,
The caterpillar in the apple,
Eating all the insides out,
Is like all the animals
They're being dragged out
They won't survive if we are to
Have a future.

Gemma Frisby (13)
Uppingham Community College

WHAT IF . . .

What if the government was no more
And the future horizon everyone saw?

What if the children had their say
But men and women went away?

If the sun and moon spoke out loud
And had conversation with the clouds.

What if all mankind was extinct
And all the planets were linked?

What if one day all this came
And everyone was exactly the same?

What if it was a lonely cold world
But I'd rather be back at home?

Leah Jennings (12)
Uppingham Community College

FUTURE SCHOOLS

Will there be teachers in future schools,
Or will there be robots giving the rules?

There could be computers on everyone's desks,
We would use them for work and even our tests.

Will we have rockets instead of cars,
Would we shoot up to school on Mars?

So . . .
Up into space we will go,
What will happen I don't know.

Katy Spedding (12)
Uppingham Community College

THE PARTY GIRL

The lights are bright and blazing
A girl walks in and I start gazing.

At this beautiful young girl
Standing in the light she shines like a pearl.

The drinks start going around the place
She looked very nice with her rosy face.

Her hair was golden with a hint of brown
I asked her out but she turned me down.

I go home feeling very glum
While my heartbeats for her like a drum.

I get home and get ready for bed
Still hearing the music beat in my head.

Robert Meeney (13)
Uppingham Community College

FUTURE VOICES AND WHAT THEY SAY

Future voices whispering in my ear,
Future voices they're so very clear,
They tell me there are holidays to the moon
And they'll be coming your way very soon.

Robots will be doing every chore,
So we can watch TV more and more.
The sun will always be out
There will never be a rain cloud about.

So what future voices are trying to say,
A day in the future will never be grey.

Kylie Muller (12)
Uppingham Community College

WAR AND PEACE

Once I had a dream,
About war and peace it seems.
I thought I saw people
Talking, night and day.
Government, parliament
From every country.
Kings and Queens from
Every state.
People, people, everywhere,
All talking.
Trying to make peace with
Everybody, not war!
One night I had a dream
About war and peace it seems.

Charlotte Swift (12)
Uppingham Community College

LIFE IS LIKE A STONE

Life is like a stone,
One day you get walked on,
Then the next, you get left on the side,
You are living a losing battle,
You may get eroded,
In a flash flood of unhappiness
And swept away with a raging river,
But sometimes,
The sun shines down on you
And warms you.
The crystals inside you shine,
Making you happy once again.

Hayley Nix (13)
Uppingham Community College

THE DESERT'S STORY

Deserts are like a lonely child
They just sit and wait,
But when something comes,
It springs with life,
A friend, the rain, a cloud.

The desert is like a lonely child
It's life is nearly nil,
It's blank and grey, every day
Like a blurred picture.

The desert is like a lonely child
It's always sad and glum
The life that lies beneath
Is never seen for fun.

Sam Horner (13)
Uppingham Community College

FUTURE VOICES

Lurking, twirling by the door,
Is there someone there at all?
I'm freaking out, please go away,
Who wants the shadow to stay?
Not me, no way!
I could dream of that another day,
Go away, shadow, go!
Who leaves the shadow on the floor,
Who is that lurking round the door?
The stream is sparkling in the moon.
Oh please go away shadow,
And very soon!

Terri Lynch (12)
Uppingham Community College

FUTURE VOICES SAY GOODBYE

Can you hear the birds sing?
Can you hear the bell ring?
Can you hear the people shout
And do you know what about?

Can you see the sun and moon?
Did you hear the great big boom?
In people's hearts, in people's minds,
Which could destroy all mankind.

Children playing, children laughing
Families destroyed, earthquake starting.
Listening to the people crying
Hundreds and thousands of people dying.

Children are now orphans and families are lost
People were happy at no such cost,
But now that all the world had changed,
They all say that God's to blame.

Two days later it starts again
An earthquake in the wind and rain,
All the people lying dead
In a cold, icy, lonely bed.

What will the future on earth be?
It could be ruled by you or me.
The future voices who are they?
No one, for they have passed away.

Did you hear the people cry
For future voices say goodbye.

Sonia Whitsey (12)
Uppingham Community College

TO A NEW DAY OF SOUND

To a new day of sound
To a new day of sound.

Animals wake up yawning,
The trees rustling in the wind,
The forest moving lightly,
The birds begin to sing.

To a new day of sound,
To a new day of sound.

The forests now awake
And now full of life,
Listening to everything around it,
Watching the slightest movement,
Of the forest animals wandering.

To a new day of sound,
To a new day of sound.

Sounds of all sorts,
Of birds and animals,
Rustling bushes and trees,
The wind howling.

To a new day of sound,
To a new day of sound.

When night comes,
All is quiet again,
The forest is asleep,
Until morning comes.

Louise Pickwoad (13)
Uppingham Community College

HOMELESS

A dustbin is like a three course meal
For a homeless person.

Each time they are hungry
They go to a 24 hour restaurant
In search of a tasty meal.

There's a cafe on every corner,
A canteen on every block,
A take out under each lamp-post
And a bar behind each shop.

A shop doorway is like a five star hotel
For a homeless person.

Each time they are tired
They find a B & B (but without breakfast)
And sleep in a four post bed of cardboard.

There's a hotel in every street,
A home in every town,
A B & B each city
And a bedroom on each estate.

Charlotte Neild (14)
Uppingham Community College

DANCE OF THE HEAVENS

A silent maiden in her wedding gown,
Features paled and drawn in expectation
Her sad face ever turned towards
Her loved one: Earth.

Gliding round his obstinate form,
Trying to distract his attention from
Sun, the one Earth has eyes only for,
The brilliant one besides whom moon's beauty pales.

She is drawn towards the bulk of his body,
Never able to break the attraction between
Herself and the uncaring Earth.
Who, for aeons, has ignored her attempts at love.

Still through the years, the dance goes on,
Silent figures watching each other,
Earth's adoration for the haughty sun,
The hopeless love of moon for Earth.

Anna Mackellar (14)
Uppingham Community College

FUTURE VOICES

Now anger, then hush
Now tears, then laughter
Noise always round us
But what of the future?

Will our voices go on?
Will they sound the same?
Will we hear our favourite song?
Will we call our best friend's name?
We want to laugh, to dance to songs
We want to remain the same.

The future is bringing new voices
Computers, robots, metallic sounds
No feelings in these new voices
Just flat and empty all around.

We don't want to lose our voices,
We don't want to lose that sound,
We want our voices to carry on
Until there is silence all around.

Summer O'Connor (13)
Uppingham Community College

COMMUNICATION IN THE YEAR 2000

Hush, be quiet, hear the whispering tone,
Of rippling wave lengths, reaching home.
Travelling silently through space and time,
Reaching Earth for us to find.

Hearing and seeing people world wide,
Means you won't need a phone glued to your side,
All talking would flow through the mind,
With gossip being yesterday's news with no crossed lines.

I read the past and days gone by,
I see the present, doesn't time fly?
But what of the future? I don't know,
You have to live it, if you want to know.

Annie Burns (12)
Uppingham Community College

WATER

A wave folded over the dark deep blue ocean,
Swishing, swirling,
And slowly drifting to shore.
The greeny, blue, white surfed edged wave
Rippled onto the golden sandy beach.
Then turned and headed down to the
Awaiting sea.
Swish!
Another wave wraps round the water
And folds over the sea.
And another,
And another,
For eternity!

Erin Garton (13)
Uppingham Community College

FUTURE VOICES

The future, I wonder
What will it be like?
Maybe flying buses
Cars and motorbikes.

The vehicles are electric
And run real swift,
They take you right up
Just like in a lift.

Boxing is really cool
Gloves are made of lead
Watch out you don't get hit
Or you will end up dead.

And then what of the cricket?
It really is quite lame,
They don't have fours or sixes
It's just not the same.

We have no books
To write on at school
We write on computers
With lasers, how cool!

Clothes have special buttons
On coats they are green,
So when you fly around at night
You can always be seen.

The future will come
And soon be here,
Nothing has changed
It's just another year.

Leon Barnes (12)
Uppingham Community College

FUTURE VOICES

The darkness of midnight,
The moonlight shines on the river,
The stars twinkle on your fingertips,
Your hair shines in the moonlight,
Your eyes sparkle like cat's eyes.

The haunted house is very spooky,
Dark corners filled with cobwebs,
Eerie rooms that hold the unexpected
And ghosts that roam the corridors,
Waiting to pounce.

All the gardens with secret doors,
The hedges cut into ghosts and animals,
Babies cry helplessly in fear,
The wind howls through the open windows
Doors bang shut as the wind blows.

People screaming as they are murdered,
Pots and pans crashing to the floor,
The piano playing by itself,
Cars rushing by, dare not stop.
I think this is what will happen in the future.

Katie Moore (12)
Uppingham Community College

FUTURE VOICES

They sit there waiting
Chewing the ends of their pencils
Fiddling with pens
Biting their nails
As the chewing gum from under the table,
Falls on their knees.
They are waiting for the sound.

The teacher stands there waiting
Ranting on
Reading passages
Calling the register
Giving out work
Marking books and drinking coffee
She's waiting for the sound.

'Pack away' the teacher says
They stand behind their chairs
'Be quiet' the teacher says,
'I'm waiting . . .'
They shuffle around
And scuff their shoes
There's a pause
Bringgg! Bringgg!
Off you go
The sound has passed,
They're waiting for the next one.

Becky Corby (11)
Uppingham Community College

MY BIG JUNGLE

When I wake up in the morning and climb down my tree,
I walk along my jungle floor where I meet my bumble bee,
After that I try to get to my spare rock which I keep inside my new furs,
But it was blocked by my wild cat which was full of lots of purrs!
So then I shooed her out of my way and lifted up my heavy rock
And I got a gigantic, big, big shock,
For a great big python stood in my way,
'Hissss' it said 'I say, I say . . . '
But before it finished I had thrown it out of the jungle
And tried to find my newest fur from my big bungle.
When the time came to go back to my tree,
I walked along the jungle floor and said 'Goodnight'
                                    to my buzzy bee
So over the hill and down round the bend,
All good things must come to an end.

Goodnight!

Laura Brant (11)
Uppingham Community College

FUTURE VOICES

Will there be,
No more poverty?
No starving, no homeless, no cruelty at all,
A world full of happiness, that's pleasurable for all.

Or a life saving pill?
So nobody's ill,
No waiting lists, no waiting rooms, no waiting together,
A world full of happiness, that's painless forever.

Or an automatic car,
No I need to travel far,
No driving tests, no seatbelts, no driving at all,
A world full of happiness, that's easy for all.

The future looks bright
Not at all tight,
No past, no present, just think of the future
And what it can hold . . .

Loretta Johnson (12)
Uppingham Community College

JUNGLE

As soon as you enter my room it's the jungle,
The door turns into some bushes.
My bed turns into a pile of leaves,
My stereo into a scary spider,
My wardrobes are like leaning trees.

My chest of drawers is a pile of logs,
The stairs in my bedroom are creepers.
My window is a gap in the trees showing light,
My shelves are a steep cliff face,
The airing cupboard, an eagle's nest!

But worst of all are the strange wild animals,
With their fierce and shining eyes.
But don't I know these furry faces,
I'm sure I have seen them before?
I know I have, they're my fluffy toys that
I keep at the end of my bed!

Alice Dawtrey (12)
Uppingham Community College

FUTURAMA

F rom the year 1999 to 2999
U nder the burning sun,
T he world has changed in this time
U ppingham has changed, it must have done
R ailways are no longer on ground but
A bove the buildings and sea.
M any things are gone even the tea cups
A nd all these things have got to be.

W andering robots going around on wheels
O perated by one machine inside them
R eally clever these things that make meals
L ove to have them around but don't love them
D on't care for them, they're only robots.

Ryan Upton-Andrew (12)
Uppingham Community College

FUTURE VOICES

5, 4, 3, 2, 1
Blast off!
We've just launched a rocket
And I'm in it.
What . . .
Can you repeat that last message
It wasn't us.
I hear a voice so loud and happy
And it's saying.
Ring, ring, rang, rang, rang
It sounds like it's dancing
And playing
And having lots of fun.

Harriet Lammie (11)
Uppingham Community College

FUTURE VOICES

Future voices float in the air:
Most people just don't care
But I listen,
I hear every whisper, every word
Flying through the air like birds.
They say that the future's bright:
I hope that they are right.
They say that money won't exist
So there will be no poor;
They say robots will do the work
And we can relax more.

I hear them speaking every night
I hope to God that they're right.

Future voices in the air,
Am I the only one that cares?

Gary Marshall (12)
Uppingham Community College

FUTURE VOICES

In the future our cars will be green,
This will make the air nice and clean,
The factories won't pollute my air,
I'll be able to see from here to there,
Video phones for one and all,
We'll be able to see whose making the call,
PC's, TV's, E-mail's and all,
All on your wrist waiting to call,
Robotic housewives who work for no fee,
While I watch the footie on TV.

Brad Clawson (11)
Uppingham Community College

BEFORE THE CHANGE

Before the change, the world was warm
But now it's bitter cold,
There are lots of young and middle aged
But no one's really old.
No houses left, no schools to learn,
It's really rather strange,
I don't remember very much
About the so called change.

They say there once were surgeries
To go to when you were poorly,
Now they just lay down and die
That can't be right, surely?
We have to fight and kill to eat,
It's the only way to live
But when all the animals have gone
There will be nothing left to give.

At night we try to get some rest
Knowing what's ahead
If we don't protect each other
We are sure to be dead.
Every corner you go around,
You have to do with care,
Never wander on your own,
Always in a pair.

I heard a man the other day
Talking about the past
And how they just assumed
That all the good would last
Apparently the grass was green
The skies were nice and bright
So much, so that in the day
Everything was light.

Jon Handyside (13)
Uppingham Community College

I LIVE IN A BEDROOM . . . I THINK

Wake up in my bedroom, well
I think it's a bedroom.
I think that's my bed over
there, or it could be some
jagged rocks.
There is my desk, or is it
seaweed?
Are they my slippers or are
they some fish?
My wardrobe looks like the
wreck of a ship
And my drawers are a
treasure chest.
In the middle of the room
there is a mess, but I think
it's coral.
I don't live in a bedroom I live
Underwater!

Barnaby Allan (11)
Uppingham Community College

FUTURE VOICES

Less pollution,
Hover cars,
Robots that talk,
Trips to Mars.

Better computers,
Safer planes,
G M Foods,
Uncrashable trains.

The future,
The place to be,
Wish I was there,
That's it from me.

Matthew Stevens (11)
Uppingham Community College

MILLENNIUM

The millennium is coming,
It will be here soon,
Some people think it will bring happiness,
Some think a monsoon.

Some people it scares,
Some people it excites,
If we don't hurry up
It will give us a fright.

The Millennium Bug is eating
All of our IT
He likes a keyboard for his snack
And a printer for his tea.

Daniel Halliday (11)
Uppingham Community College

IN THE FUTURE

I once had a dream,
Of the future,
It may seem,
When cars hovered in the sky,
Ever so high.
Where all sorts of technology
Roamed the streets
And those dreadful schools,
Became extinct.
Where dinosaurs lived again
Yikes!
And . . .

I suddenly woke up,
My dream,
Had just begun . . .

Chloe Atkinson (11)
Uppingham Community College

FUTURE VOICES

It was early morning when we heard some voices
And didn't know where they were coming from,
We didn't take any notice after we had our breakfasts.
We just got on with our days work, then again later the
Same day we heard these
Voices calling us again and again.
It was if our great grandchildren were calling us to the
Future to be with them all times.
They were our future voices who kept calling us,
It got fainter and fainter and eventually disappeared
Into the distance.

Sarah-Jane-Ann Giddings (11)
Uppingham Community College

FUTURE VOICES

I'm told about the future,
How cars will fly through the air,
I'm told about the future,
How animals never
Become rare,
I'm told about the future,
How no one needs to
Go to school.
A computer chip will
Be put in your hand,
Now that would
Be so cool.
I'm told about the future
How lasers open food
Tins,
I'm told about the future,
How fishes swim with
No fins,
I'm told about the future,
In more ways than one,
Why can't this century
Have gone,
I'm told about the future,
But what I really can't
Understand,
Is why school dinners
Will never be banned!

Alex Wyatt (11)
Uppingham Community College

FUTURE VOICES - LISTEN

Listen! What can you hear?
The pop of beech seed burst beneath my feet
As I walk to the bus stop
Oh a cool, crisp, autumnal morning.

Listen! What can you hear?
The crunch of fallen leaves
As I kick them on my way home
On a cool, crisp, autumnal afternoon.

Listen! What can you hear?
The grating of my boots
As I slide down the icy road
On my way to the bus stop.

Listen! What can you hear?
The bark of hounds
As I walk past the stables
In the big yard
On my way home.

Listen! What can you hear?
The panting of my friend's dog
Straining on its lead
As I walk to the bus stop.

Listen! What can you hear?
The laughter and chatter
Of the school children of tomorrow -
The future voices.

Robyn Sampson (12)
Uppingham Community College

MY BEDROOM

Bleep! Bleep! Bleep! Bleep!
My eyes open, I'm a star.
I dream of Hollywood and here I am.
My bedroom's amazing
It's like a movie star's.
Stars and stripes on my bedcover,
Bright yellow inflatable chair,
Sky Digital, Surround Sound TV
Luxurious, cosy and warm,
It makes me feel sleepy.
I get my breakfast, but I eat
it in my room, because it is just
so nice.
I think my room is the best in the house.
The rest of the house isn't very
tidy,
But my room is!

Joshua Mann (11)
Uppingham Community College

FUTURE VOICES

Future voices calling out,
For those in need and doubt,
For those who need a little help,
Future voices coming out in the next millennium!

Future voices are calling out,
For you and me to sing and shout,
To dance and move and run about,
Future voices are calling, calling, calling out,
For the next millennium!

Pippa Leslie (11)
Uppingham Community College

MY FOOTBALL GROUND

When I wake up in the morning
I hear millions of people cheering
And I feel somebody shaking me
'John, John, wake up.'
I sleep in the goals
and the corner flags
are the corners of my bed.
I get up
The morning comes
Step over the sidelines
I then sit down in
the manager's box to
have a cup of tea.
I stand up and yell
at the players on TV
as if I am the manager.
I then hear the final whistle
being blown by my sister.

John McKie (11)
Uppingham Community College

CHILDREN OF TODAY

The children of today
Are the voices of the future
At the moment our lives
Are decided by the majority
Of other people.
Whatever we do,
Affects the world.

Hugo de Verteuil (11)
Uppingham Community College

YOUR HEART

Your heart is not a plaything,
Your heart is not a toy,
But if you want it broken,
Then give it to a boy.
It is a living thing,
It has a heart of its own,
Your body is its worker,
Your body is its home.
Life without a heart,
Would be like life without dreams,
Life without colour and life without a theme,
Your heart keeps you alive
And holds all of your emotions
And most of all, it holds all your true love
And devotions.

Charlotte Carr (13)
Uppingham Community College

THE OCEAN

My bedroom is like a swimming pool,
My bedroom is like the blue ocean,
If I tipped my bedroom upside down
I wonder what I would see?

The ceiling would be the white sand
And the floor would be the bright sky.
The bed is a big whale, the chest of drawers
Would be like the little fish floating by.
The wardrobe is like a ship wreck that sank
In the World War.

Alan Thackray (11)
Uppingham Community College

THE MONKEY SISTER!

As the monkey walks
Through the door of my bedroom
You can already tell she's annoying.
The tedious, aggravating, little toerag
Just sits and views the world.
She rises up and ambles over,
Now it's tugging on my hair,
'Get off and go away' I cry.
'You mischievous, cheeky, noisy,
Bothersome, irritating chimp!'
She strolls along and sits back down
What's that exasperating ape doing now?
Chucking things at me that's what she's doing.
How troublesome, tiring and misbehaving is that?
Luckily mother monkey comes and
Takes her to bed.

Hannah Murdock (12)
Uppingham Community College

STADIUM ROOM

My room is Old Trafford, the seat's full of crowds
Players line the walls,
I sleep in the commentary box and commentate
The matches.
My brother is down in the tunnel
And takes the sent-off away,
The light is the floodlights that shine
Down on the turf.
The windows are the directors' boxes
With people filling them up.

Jonathan Byron (11)
Uppingham Community College

My Battlefield

When I come home from school, the battle is still raging on,
Damaged machines on the floor, the screeching of the planes
As they are shot down, breaking into Lego bits on the floor.
Little people running around my feet as I go into the full battle.
Enemy bases around my feet, I tread on one and out
Come Lego men shouting as I trample their base into little Lego bits.
I get to my bed and on top is a look out post with
A group of Lego soldiers.
A plane comes screeching over and the ongoing hum of the
Machine guns as they fire at it from the look out tower.
Then everything goes silent as Mum shouts up the stairs,
'Tidy your room up!'

Sam Webster (11)
Uppingham Community College

Bed Forest

I enter the room
The bedroom was a rainforest,
The toys were animals,
A massive tree has jumped up and smashed the ceiling,
There is a lake right where my desk used to be,
It's almost as if where my lamp is, or where it used to
Be, there's a reflection from the moon.
The creaking of the floor had become owls hooting and
Monkeys howling.
I climb a tree,
My room comes back from the deep
I am hanging on the light-shade.

Shaun Bennett (11)
Uppingham Community College

MY BEDROOM

When I walk through the door,
It's like a battlefield in World War Two
I look over to my bed,
The bed looks like a bomber,
The telly is a tank,
The bureau's a pile of bayonets,
The mirror's a machine gun,
My carpet's covered in corpses,
The curtain's a cargo net,
The piles of books are my sandbags,
The radiator's there to reinforce,
The dog basket's full of land mines,
The food bowl is a hat.

Anthony Bland (11)
Uppingham Community College

MY BEDROOM

Each night in the basement of my house,
With my little friend the mouse,
We retire to the ocean and there await
The commotion.

We lie awake on the old wooden boat
For the fishes to swim, but then begin
To realise that the light has now gone so dim.

Now feeling, oh so sick! The tide begins
To bubble and kick on the
Verge of going under, it certainly
Makes me think, oh what a blunder!

Steven Bennett (11)
Uppingham Community College

Bedroom In A Sink

The walls are like the bluish sides of a sink,
and the clothes on the floor
are like the bits of gunk
that stick to the sink even after you clean it.

The bed is like a plug that makes
creeping noises
every time you move it.

The lamp is like a light
that shines upon the sink
drying it.

The shelves are like the taps
hanging there, prettily shining.

My drawers are like a white patch
upon the sink
when someone tipped glue on it.

You sit there in this transfixed state
until your mum shouts in,
'Clean that room!'

Siân Davies (11)
Uppingham Community College

My Bedroom

As you walk in my room,
The sun is bright,
You have to rub in sun lotion,
With all your might.

My bed is a shell,
My wardrobe a chest
Which is full of jewels
Gold and the rest.

My desk is a crab,
Creeping across the floor.
My light is an oyster
And so is my door.

My shelves are branches
On top of the tree,
With thousands upon thousands
Of little book leaves.

Jack Blake (11)
Uppingham Community College

MY BEDROOM

The fluffy pillow cloud softens all of my worries,
My room keeps changing as I fall asleep,
Clouds float around soothing all of my thoughts,
While the cool breeze passes over me,
Dark clouds close in.
The bookshelves enclose all my secrets,
My personal items fade into memories,
The CD player softly plays favourite tunes,
Fox toys protect me from devils in the sky,
Different places are all around me,
While I sleep,
Peace and quiet conquer my world,
A wicker basket holds the past,
Books store thoughts of the future,
A magic carpet is ready to fly,
Cries of animals can be heard down below,
The eye of a window looks out,
Yet no one can see me,
I'm only a child not yet fully grown,
My bedroom is me and also my home.

Emily Nix (11)
Uppingham Community College

BEDROOM IN SPACE

I woke up
For school and
Went to get
Dressed and my
Uniform was floating.
So I went
To get washed.
I turned on
The tap and
The water flew
Up so I
Thought for a
Minute, then I
Had an idea.
Go back to
Bed, so I
Did. My bed
Was a spaceship
Which was
Powered to float, then someone
Turned on the
Moon and star
Lights and said
'The water is
Everywhere.'

Craig Bamber (11)
Uppingham Community College

CLUCKING LIKE A CHICKEN BUT ROARING LIKE A DRAGON

Just like a chicken,
Clucking and pecking,
Starting to get broody,
Sitting on an egg of evilness,
She protects her unborn baby,
With her stare of the devil!

As you get closer, the feathers start
to ruffle,
And the farmyard animal,
Once quite normal *squawks* again
and again.

The poultry now a fire-breathing
Dragon!
Red eyes flaming with anger,
Scales rippling down her back,
Her mouth opens as if to swallow you,
Teeth so sharp and spiky,
Sharp enough to cut through steel.

You feel as though you are getting
smaller and smaller,
Then suddenly she turns,
And goes back into her dark cold
Lair!

Poppy Burgess (12)
Uppingham Community College

LIVING IN A TRENCH

Living in a trench.
Trudging through the waste.
New belongings discarded every day,
Cramped up in a tiny space.
The only source of light,
A tiny lighter stuck in the wall of mud.
A top bunk covered in letters and card
Put together like a soft white quilt.
Pieces of glass stuck with gum,
                    to form a mirror.
Jewellery hits the ground with such a thud.
There doesn't seem too much life anymore,
All killed by trying to live in
                    my bedroom!

Georgie Beard
Uppingham Community College

THE SHOP LIKE ROOM

As I walk into my bedroom
I'm in a department store . . .
My clothes all neat hanging on rails
My shoes lined up in pairs on the floor
And my bed is a sofa to be sold in the sales.
Bears and Beanie Babies, cosy and warm.
Books, games, instruments, TV and radio alarm.
The desk is the check out all clean, the floor all
        Clear, no rubbish in the bin . . .
At least this is what it looks like
When my mum's been in!

Ellie Lane (12)
Uppingham Community College

THE BRIGHT-EYED SQUIRREL!

On a crisp, frosty morning as the sun breaks through,
before man has risen and the grass still holds dew,
A small bright-eyed squirrel whose work is all done
scampers up and down trees. I'm sure just for fun.
As the sun keeps on rising and man starts to stir,
the squirrel can feel the warmth on his fur -
He'll soon start his hoarding and making his dray
to be warm and happy on a long winter's day.
He has to work hard and he has to work fast
to make sure he's secure as he has in the past.
As man awakens and the noise starts to grow,
the bright-eyed squirrel knows it's time to go.
He will sleep a deep sleep all safe and sound
dreaming of acorns that are hidden in the ground.

Becky Williams (12)
Uppingham Community College

MY BEDROOM IS . . .

I describe my bedroom as an underwater city.
My bed would be a gigantic shark, swimming
                        amongst the reeds.
My table is a mermaid's palace,
And my mirror is the clear blue sea.
My carpet is the ocean bed, beautiful and clean
The tassels on my rug become the reeds.
My light is the sun, shimmering in the sky above me.
My wardrobes are the caverns and large rocks,
And my bin, well my bin, is an old shipwreck.

Fiona Mackellar (11)
Uppingham Community College

MY ROOM IS A JUNGLE

My bed is a hammock,
Strung from two trees
The leaves keep me warm
In the cold winter breeze.

My desk is a rock,
Big, grey and round,
It's useful for dumping stuff on
I've found!

My wardrobe is a waterfall
Gushing down
It's so big, you can hear it
In the next town!

My rug is a swamp
In the middle of the jungle,
But, into it,
I must not tumble!

My room is a jungle
But I don't mind
I've made friends with the animals,
And they're really kind!

Abby Gwynne (11)
Uppingham Community College

THE BULLY

The bully waits in the shadows of the school corridors
With a sly evil smile on his face, as the young innocent
victim hops nervously around the corner.

Immediately the bully sees his chance and prowls
towards his victim with his large padded feet.

The victim whimpers as he's pinned against the locker
its small stubby hind legs dangling above the floor.
He's frozen in terror while the bully sweeps his fiery, bushy tail
and strokes his long slender whiskers. He snarls
wickedly showing his small white pointed teeth.

They stare transfixing each other's eyes when
large familiar paw steps come from around the corner.
'Hey you get off him!'
A loud bellowing voice shouts. The bully instantly drops
The victim onto the ground and casually saunters off
Down the corridor.

The victim twitched his small button nose and
Brushes his whiskers,
Trying to hold back the lonely tears, he glanced
Back down the corridor and sadly wiggled his
Cotton wool like tail as he cautiously hops away.

Connie Dickson (12)
Uppingham Community College

MY BEDROOM

My bedroom is like paradise -
When I walk in it I see
a desert room with palm trees and pyramids
I have a big poster of my favourite actor
and when I look, it springs to life.
My two camels look at me as if to say
'What are you doing?'
My palm trees hover over me to see what
I am doing, they keep me shaded from my hot
burning sunroof.
My pyramids are old, ancient and grey,
it's like they just stand there and watch me.
My bedroom all round is brill,
like I said, it's like *paradise.*

Leah Thompson (11)
Uppingham Community College

THE LANDMINE ROOM

As you come into my house,
And you go up the stairs,
You come into my landmine room,
Alive with clicks and whirrs.
My bed is the detonator,
And lots of little bits
Of metals, plastics, wires, elastic,
They are all my favourites.
Then as I lie resting in bed,
The whirring of machines
Resound in my mechanical mind,
The laboratory of my dangerous dreams . . .

Lluis Mather (11)
Uppingham Community College

Sky!

I wake up and I am still in the
nice, warm, cosy fluffy cloud,
The clouds part and the sun comes
shining through, keeping me
nice and warm,
I want to go back to sleep but the
planes are stopping me by
making a horrible racket,
I manage to get back to sleep and
I am woken by a bird tweeting
in my ear,
I look around and all I can see
is blue, blue and blue, and a little
bit of greeny black below me.

Sam Stillman (12)
Uppingham Community College

Corby Tip

My room is like Corby tip,
the bed is like a wrecked car,
curtains are like the old clothes.
My floor is like all of it mashed together.
My walls have got waste paper on them.
My CDs are all over the mashed stuff.
Every day the tip pile gets higher
and higher with magazines and school homework.
My TV and videos like rotten pieces of cardboard
and my PlayStation like a plastic bag with all
the games scattered around like pieces of chewed paper.
My schoolbag like a mouldy sandwich
and my clothes covered in moss.

Leanne Robbins (11)
Uppingham Community College

MY DISCO ROOM

I come home from school, I open the door to my room.
I hear music, I can see my teddies dancing.
My rocking horse is rocking, all my clothes have fallen off it!
My music player is alive.
My beanie baby is next to it changing the CDs.
My wardrobe is reflecting the lights.
I drop my bag on the floor and start dancing,
I trip over some of my shoes
'Ow!'
My mother walks up the stairs, I am still on the floor!
My mum opens the door then the music stops
'Are you OK?'
'Yes' I said.
She shuts the door, the music starts again,
The disco carries on.

Heather Shears (11)
Uppingham Community College

MY CITY GROUND

My bedroom's like the City ground,
The players sitting on the bed as if it was a bench.
The desk is like a camera box,
The TV like a commentary box.
The radio sets the atmosphere,
It's just the cheers from the crowd.
I'm now going home to my bedroom
To see the FA Cup Final.
My carpet's like the clean grass,
My light like the floodlights - glittering on the floor.

Richard Mills (12)
Uppingham Community College

CAFÉ TIME

I wake in the morning with a milkshake by my side,
with waiters roller-skating all around inside.
Breakfast bars with cashiers cashing in money,
tables and chairs all around, menus filled with what we sell:

	Coffee
	Cakes
and	*Chocolate milkshakes,*
	Tea and *biscuits*
and	*Burgers in buns,*
	Fish and chips
and	*Waffles with syrup.*

'Yum! Yum! I love to eat them.

Hannah Southerington (11)
Uppingham Community College

MY BEDROOM IS LIKE A BOMB SITE

My bedroom is like a bomb site.
The light hanging from my ceiling is like
a bomber that has just dropped a bomb
straight through my floor.
The junk that is thrown all over my room
is like wreckage left after the bomb has dropped.
My lamp is like a torch shining in the light.
My bed is like a rowing boat retreating from the enemy.
My carpet is like the scraps of dirt left over from the war.
My wardrobe's like the gates of a death camp with
                        dead people inside,
And my door is like a gateway to freedom.
                        Hooray!

Emma Cole (11)
Uppingham Community College

CANDYFLOSS

Sweet sticky candyfloss,
Surrounded by thick pink moss.
Straggly sugar strings on the floor,
Something's hanging that seems very sore.
Soft fluffy cotton wool,
A dangling thread ready to pull.

Big, bouncy puffiness at the back of my room,
A surprise sweetie in an enclosed tomb.
Soft, squiggly, silky layers of colour,
Sparkling and bright not faded and duller.

More like strings of sugar tangled together,
The wonderful pink softness forever.
More like a cloud of pink about to rain,
It has a lovely sweet name.

Looks like it's come out of a big bad mixer,
In huge holes there is a big balding trickster.
The top of the tower has gone mouldy white,
Make my way to that enormous height.
Trendy and artful in designer pink,
A place to relax and somewhere to think.

Alice Cocks (11)
Uppingham Community College

MY JUNGLE ROOM

As I walked into the jungle of a bedroom
I saw the wardrobe representing a tree,
and the tiger disguised as a dressing table
was waiting to pounce on me.

I moved to the left, stepping onto the leaves,
my mum's always telling me to pick up these.
I ran to the bunk bed and climbed up the ladder high,
and realised I was on a elephant's back
almost touching the sky.

The tops of the trees were all I could see,
oh, and the tiger, was looking at me.
I hid under my quilt which was an elephant's ear,
here I was safe with nothing to fear.

In the morning I awoke with the sun shining through,
the tiger was asleep all covered with dew.
I slid down the trunk of the elephant and crunched on
the leaves and all I could see was the grass and mud
and the tiger was still looking at me.

When I walked out of my room,
I suddenly realised that my jungle was a dream.

Lucy Parkin (11)
Uppingham Community College

MY BEDROOM

My bedroom is like a crowded beach.
I share it with my sister Holly.
Our clothes are like towels littering the
yellow sand with many colours.
Soon my bedroom will be a deserted
beach when I have a room to myself.
This beach will have clear blue sea
and unspoilt sand.
The walls will be blue with white
framed pictures for waves.
The warm beige carpets will let
my feet sink in and cover my toes.
My bed will be driftwood and my
pillows - dolphins, sheets - turtles and coral.
I'll sleep on the driftwood and dream
on the dolphins.
I'll wake refreshed and alive.
The gulls will be calling.
'Harriet, you'll be late for school.'
I'll open my doors from my beach
heaven, and back into the real world.

Harriet Marcus (11)
Uppingham Community College

MY JUNGLE BEDROOM

As I walked towards my normal bedroom,
well, that's what I thought it was,
I opened the door and what did I see,
a bedroom full of chimpanzee.
What was that beside my bed, a flea,
or could it be the smallest of bumblebee?
My bedroom was a mess, but not of books or clothes.
It was of trees with leaves.
There were not only chimpanzees but elephants,
tigers, snakes and the strangest of creepy-crawlies
a'crawling all over me.
I went towards my cupboard, to find something to wear.
But to my surprise, the cupboard was bare.
When I turned around, to my surprise, I saw a
chimp come flying by.
But that is not just why he was strange,
he had on my pants and my socks in his cage.
Not only that, a snake was slithering in and out of my hat.
I was going to a disco in half-an-hour, but I couldn't find
my make-up and time was passing by.
I had to find it quick and I mean, quick!
I turned around as I did before, and as usual something
was strange and this time it was the tiger.
It had on lipstick, blusher and was drinking cider.
There was also a parrot sitting on my lamp.
I sat down and it moved to sit on my lap.
Now to settle this poem in the easiest way, is just to say . . .
My bedroom is a mess,
     a mad and a fun place to be every day.

Leona Friar (11)
Uppingham Community College

I LOVE HIM

I love him,
but he doesn't know.
We're really good friends,
I can't let it show.

Whenever I see him
I feel like dying.
It hurts inside,
I just feel like crying.

It's so hard to keep
my secret love,
I might just send
a loving dove.

Christie Greenway (14)
William Bradford Community College

THE SNOWMAN

I woke up this morning with a bit of a dizzy head,
And then all I could think of was to get up out of bed.
I took a few paces forward and then felt like dropping dead.
I looked out of the window, it was snowing!
I opened the drawer and put on some clothes,
If I hadn't I would have probably froze.
I ran down the stairs and opened the door
And there was a snowman so still and so sure.
I asked him his name and he said it was Fred,
I would have probably guessed as it was written on his head.
I asked him if he was cold as he had no clothes,
He replied, 'Snowmen aren't meant to keep warm.'

Glyn Parnell (14)
William Bradford Community College

LIFE IS LIKE A ROLLER-COASTER

Life is like a roller-coaster, full of ups and downs.
For the start of the ride, you are brought to life.
As you climb your merry way up the 100 ft drop,
You're going through school, not a worry in the world.
You reach the top, you can see for miles around
As you wait anxiously for that certain unmissable drop.
You've left school and got no money.
As you carry on down,
You think things can't get any worse,
Then you're on the way up as you get a job.
As you carry on round, you lose momentum.
You retire and live on your pension
And finally after all these ups and downs
The ride finally ends,
In your death.

Thomas Blake (15)
William Bradford Community College

IMAGES OF WAR

I crawl out of the trench in my mind,
I cannot see what I am trying to find.
There are no more beautiful sights,
No more battles and no more vicious fights.
The scenic landscape which sits here and there,
The mountains, the forests and the Somme are now bare,
There is as I walk a mass grave of men
That fought and screamed and died there and then,
This place where the battle is lost and won
Is now nothing more than oblivion!

Jamie Leigh (17)
William Bradford Community College

A DREAM

A dream is a thought,
left in the back of our minds,
woken when you sleep.
Meaningful or meaningless
everyone has ideas.
If dreams could talk to us,
what would they say,
would they tell the truth or lies?
Maybe our conscience is part of a dream,
or maybe our dreams are reality.
We imagine our friends,
we imagine our lives,
and they come true in our minds.
I've thought this for many years,
as you will think this for years to come,
your imagination has run wild.

Laura Bateman (15)
William Bradford Community College

LOST LOVE

Last night I had a dream, we were together,
how real it seemed.
Walking in the rain and we never got wet,
it was just too real to forget.
Every corner that we turned
we saw people that we knew,
smiling just at me and you.
I woke up this morning and you were gone,
I just don't know how I can carry on.

Daniel Malkin (14)
William Bradford Community College

LOVE IS LIFE . . . TO ME!

Love is life . . . to me,
Life is love . . . to see,
Me and you together we will be,
'Cause love is like a tree that grows,
Bigger, bigger and bigger still.

Love is life . . . to me.
Love is ups and downs
And round abouts,
This gives me doubts.

Love is life . . . to me,
O don't you see
That you and me
Will be together for eternity.

Tara Pickering (15)
William Bradford Community College

DOLPHINS

Dolphins are beautiful animals, swimming in the sea,
Blue, grey and silver, looking around at me.
Jumping high in the air, in the shape of an arc,
Friendly and loving, nothing like a shark.

Their coats shine like silver, glimmering in the sun,
Jumping through hoops, playing with balls,
Trying to have fun.
Look at their fearless eyes, glistening in the moonlight,
Contented, happy and carefree,
Don't worry, they won't bite.

Lois Shaw (14)
William Bradford Community College

OBSESSION

Every time I see you, you seem to run and hide,
Every time I see you, you don't notice me,
I spend my money on you but you don't seem to care.

When I see you standing in front of me,
It all seems to be irrelevant,
                    The waiting,
                    The longing,
                    The needing,
You take over my mind, you override my emotions.
I feel numb when I see you because in a way,
I love you.

I look into your eyes but you never look into mine,
I feel like you are going to be stolen away from me.
I have only spoken to you once,
But it didn't seem like you wanted to reply.
I love you in a way,
But you don't know I exist.

I love you so.
To live, I only need one piece of knowledge,
Will you ever be mine?

Philippa Ward (14)
William Bradford Community College

US

I see two stars in summer's night,
Hovering, lost in blinding light,
Each so dim in heaven's net,
So each remains, as yet unmet.

But fortune moves in strangest ways,
It lengthens nights, it shortens days,
May this night end and day begin
And bring two young lovers back again.

Emelie Kleen-Barry (14)
William Bradford Community College

WHAT A TEAM

Leicester City are my team,
I wish they would win the league,
but sometimes I feel it's just a distant dream.

Martin O'Neill - what a man,
if he can't do it, nobody can.
He's won the cup and taken us into Europe,
maybe that dream will come true,
and the ribbons on the cup will be blue.

With a team of hard-workers the league will be ours,
or will it, will it? I ask myself.
Week in, week out we perform,
but is it enough to reach that mighty platform?

With a squad of internationals,
we know we can beat the best,
even with not a lot of rest.

With players like Heskey, Guppy and Izzet
who are all capable of playing for England,
it feels as though we will soon reach the promised land.

Each day brings new things and new hopes,
but please, one day, let it be the league.

Nicholas Greenhill (14)
William Bradford Community College

BLUE IS . . .

Blue is the sound of a waterfall gushing down the rocks,
or blue can be sad or cold when you are all alone.
Blue is the colour of a sky on a hot summer's day,
and it also is the colour of the sea.

Blue is the colour of jeans and jumpers,
you see the colour blue everywhere you look.
On the motorway, you see blue cars and lorries.
Blue is water when it is frozen
and blue is glaciers trickling down the mountain slopes.

Blue is my favourite colour,
way better than pink.
Blue is the colour of some beautiful marine fish,
swimming in the blue waters.
Blue is Christmas Day
when it is snowing outside,
but inside is warm and dry.

Lindsey Gibson (14)
William Bradford Community College

FISH IN A BOWL

I won a fish
A few years ago,
All it does is go round and round
In its bowl.
I think I called it something,
But I can't remember it any more,
Now it's dead
And I've got a Tamagotchi instead.

Gavin Spence (14)
William Bradford Community College

FOOTBALL

A superb game in any language.
Soccer, Fussball, Foot, or as we say, Football,
a sport watched by hundreds of millions of
the top flight fans.
Take our Carling Premier League,
filled with star players like
Owen, Beckham and Yorke,
and of course the great teams,
Man U, Villa, Liverpool and Arsenal
all paying millions of pounds
for the best players in the world,
Suker, Hasselbaink, Carlos and Ronaldo too.
All the fans sing a song to you.
Football,
a superb game in any language,
in the year of the finest.

Richard Tweed (14)
William Bradford Community College

SUNDAY DINNER

Have you ever thought about the lonely cow
that stands in the field?
Do you think she knows that she's
to be our next meal?
The farmer feeds her to stop her
from getting thinner,
do you think she knows that she's
to be someone's dinner?
All this murder, I think I might turn 'veggie'
then again, one more burger can't hurt.

Kevin Ward (15)
William Bradford Community College

WHAT'S BEYOND THE CLOUDS?

As I gaze up at the light blue sky
I watch the clouds as they float by,
Some make up figures,
Some are big and some are small,
But others have no shape at all.
I wonder to myself,
What's beyond those mysterious clouds?
Is it a land of enchantment
With buttercups and fairies,
Or is it outer space
Where the planets hover around
In the thick, black sky,
Naked to the human eye?
When the night falls
The stars come out,
I watch them as they twinkle about,
Or maybe there is nothing!
Nothing,
Only emptiness.

Wendy Burton (15)
William Bradford Community College

THE SEA

The white horses are playing,
Running to the sand.
They crash against the cliffs
All across the land.

The horses are sleeping,
Quiet and still,
Sound asleep.
People can go in at their own will.

The horses awake, they're hungry,
They run up to the shore
To get some food,
After that they're in a bad mood.

So they start galloping
On to the shore,
Grabbing the pebbles
And taking them out
To sea even more.

Rebecca Faulks (14)
William Bradford Community College

RECIPE FOR FOOTBALL

Take 22 sweaty, greasy men
Add two linesmen and one ref,
Take them to a stadium
Watch and wait for 45 minutes
Of fouling, bad language, spitting,
Kicking, punching and 500 hundred
Thousand fans screaming out for their team
Take out and let it cool for 15 minutes,
Then put back on a higher heat.
More fouling, bad language, spitting,
Kicking, punching and 500 thousand
Fans on their feet, screaming, shouting
louder for another 45 minutes.
Maybe if you want to spice it up even more
Add a pinch of overtime or sudden death,
Or if you want a really good show, penalties,
For if you do, you will be begging for more.

Lee Cobley (14)
William Bradford Community College

A WOODLAND END

Whilst wandering under a winter daybreak,
A vivid image came to sight,
So weak, balancing on the icy breeze,
Fading silhouette kept visible by fresh light.

Untrusting, timid, something had chilled her to her soul.
Her voice was thick with dread.
Soft lips, frozen blue, rimmed in green
A warning in what she said.

Something drew her into the wood.
She tried to stop and stare,
Like a magnet it pulled her in,
Down a path that led nowhere.

Alone she walked, caged in a clouded dream.
Stumbling through a silent oak wood, across a silent stream.
In a tree, a silent bird mouthed a silent song,
Longing for life again, she tried to fight,
But something had gone wrong.

She followed through the seasons, until spring dissolved the snow.
Whichever way it twisted, she was compelled to go.
Years shot past, melted and were gone,
She convinced herself she would return,
Unknowingly forced to go on.

Back home, forgotten, a distant memory
Deep inside her feelings grew.
Her heart and blood had run cold,
Knowledge deep inside her told her, this she already knew.

Then she fell into an eerie silence,
My destiny had already been set, I screamed, ran and broke my stare,
By then the dragging feeling had also inhabited me,
I too began to wander down the path that led nowhere.

Emily Byrne (14)
William Bradford Community College

THE MIDNIGHT WANDERER

The Midnight Wanderer,
Wandering here and there.
Rain, wind or shine
He doesn't care.

He wanders through one town or another,
Not a single word does he mutter.
Anyone who may pass him by
Never looks him in the eye.

He strikes fear into your heart,
So no one talks to him, who is smart
And because he never ceases
People wonder whether he's part of another species.

You know, something not of this world,
But of a galaxy far away from here,
Where it is accustomed for them to wander in this way,
Every night and day throughout the year.

The story of this man however is just a tale
From an old book I bought from a jumble sale.

Adam Baines (14)
William Bradford Community College

ALONE

Have you ever been at some place,
Recognising everybody's face,
Until you realise that there was no one that you knew?
Have you ever walked through a room but it was more like the room
Passed around you,
Like there was a leash around your neck that pulled you through?
Not least like this is my life,
Confused, no family or wife.
I know not of my mother,
Gone is my brother.

Well I know our future was so bright,
Our whole lives were planned ahead,
Even now I can't see how our light
Seemed to burn right out, dead.
You can't take back that one mistake,
It still lives on after the life it takes
And now that you are dead and gone,
I am left to carry on.
I will never smile,
'Cause you won't stay alive for me.
Please, try to see me as a brother,
Instead of two distant strangers
And that's how it's supposed to be,
How can the devil take a brother if he's close to me?
Chances thrown,
Nothing's free.
What the hell is going on?
Cruellest dream reality.

I just live at home now
'Cause I've got no job.
Despite the agony and pain,
My will is still something that you can't confiscate.
Over my head it will always rain.

Charles Wren (14)
William Bradford Community College

A MAN'S BEST FRIEND

Dogs, dogs everywhere,
With their noses in the air.
Some are scruffy,
Some are sweet,
Some are free to roam the streets.
With their noses in the sky,
Getting patted by the passers-by.
A proud poodle prancing along,
or a sitting Dalmation howling its song.
Each is loved,
Each is hated,
Dogs with no homes have waited and waited.
Some are big,
Some are small,
Some want to be loved by all.
Dogs with no homes have no beds,
Nowhere to rest their little heads.
Dogs with homes are safe and sound,
Lost dogs go to the pound.
Waiting for someone,
Who, who?
Wishing for some lovely home to go to.

Rosanna Dawson (14)
William Bradford Community College

THE WEEK

Monday,	you wake up bursting with energy, ready for the day ahead. Then comes
Tuesday	and you're wishing that you could stay in bed.
Wednesday,	well you're half way there, but you've got to make it down the stairs.
Thursday	comes with a sleepy head. Oh how you wish you could have a rest.
Friday	comes finally, it took so long, but you wish you were still young.
Saturday,	well, what a dither, but you think long about last night and it gives you a shiver.
Sunday	is a time of rest, so when Monday comes you're looking your best.

Kerry Burrows (14)
William Bradford Community College

FOOTIE

I watch the footie on the box,
but it's better to see it live,
seeing all my heroes.
Aston Villa I go to see,
with players like Dublin, Joachim Boateng too,
singing all the songs I've learnt by heart,
eating pies and chips at half-time,
predicting what the score will be
and who will score the vital goals,
all new players coming to Villa Park
and the players I would love to sign
if I were the manager.

Liam Small (14)
William Bradford Community College

THE LAST DRAGON

In a faraway land at the time of the old,
A dragon named Merlin with wings of gold,
Lived in peace by the cool forest stream,
Day after day he would lie and dream.

He would dream of the times there had been no knights
To slay him and his friends in battles and fights,
None of his friends were left anymore,
All had been killed by the blades of knight's swords.

Now knights believed all dragons were dead,
Yet Merlin still had memories in his head
Of sword fights and battles now all that had ceased
So Merlin's life goes on now in peace.

Rachael Pearce (14)
William Bradford Community College

SUNDAYS!

Sundays are so boring,
Sundays are so bleak,
Sundays are definitely the worst
Part of the week,
With a huge Sunday dinner,
With carrots, meat and peas,
Then there's those Brussels sprouts,
They really make me heave.
It's time to do that essay,
That's due in for tomorrow,
Actually I'll just go to sleep
And find someone else's to borrow.

Naomi Morris (14)
William Bradford Community College

HAWK

On outstretched wings he flies,
mate of mine in our skies.
On sun-heated air he glides,
higher and higher, the thermal ride.
Spiralling high with wing-tip skills,
fleeting shadow on the hills.
Watchful eyes
scrutinise
far below for moving prey.
The unattentive stray away
from safety, he will see
another rodent tragedy.
Twitch, he fixes his eyes
and plummets through our skies,
folded wings stab the air,
bullet speed to get him there,
with talons sharp to pierce and crush.
No thermals here, his wings must push
Against the heavy ground,
hold fast, our meal found.
The days are long but
our chick grows strong.
Morsels of one death give life.

Lisa Varnham (14)
William Bradford Community College

DO YOU EVER WONDER?

Do you ever wonder what the future will be like,
Full of spite or full of delight
And do you ever wonder what the people will be like,
Wonder if they'll be the same, wonder if they'll change?

Sometime in the future, things may change,
No one will know, there's years to go,
But have you ever considered the future at all,
Do you care, as you won't be there?

Rebecca Sidwell (14)
William Bradford Community College

MAD

Through times of pain I will not cry,
No tears, I refuse to bleed.
Though I'm hurting down inside,
You give the strength I need.

I miss the people I used to know
And all the changes scare me,
Friends are drifting far apart,
Your bitterness will tear me.

I assumed that my life
Would be a fairy tale,
A marriage of eternal bliss,
The spirit's going stale.

Despite my agonising defence,
The hurt I try to hide
Comes seeping through the cracks I have,
The welfare will subside.

Peacefulness is breaking through,
My angel's looking down
And because of the light you give,
Maybe I won't drown.

Leanne Ashton (14)
William Bradford Community College

BULLY

Lying in bed,
the same thoughts running
through my mind,
> hurt,
> distress,
> grief,
> suffering.

The feeling in my stomach
is like it has been tied in
a thousand knots,
just wishing they will not
approach me,
> wishing,
> wishing.

Why do they hurt me,
make me suffer and torment
me?

I wanted to be friends,
not for them to hate me.
The feelings of
> affection,
> devotion,
> tenderness
seem so sweet and simple.
So why
bully me?

Sarah Robinson (14)
William Bradford Community College

THE SEASONS

Spring, the glistening cold blue sky
Weak sun gently warming the earth
And melting the trees' frosty fingers.
The ground wakes from winter's sleep.

Summer, scorching weather,
Weary people, too hot for work.
Bright blue sky, golden sunshine,
Days seem to last forever.

Autumn, a white frosty blanket
Covers the solid ground, leaves
Glide to nestle on the furrowed field.

Winter, bare trees and watery sun
With the cold, biting wind the
Thick white fog gently rolls in,
The earth sleeps again.

Thomas Bartlett (15)
William Bradford Community College

LIFE

What is life?
We all should know
that it is the flowers and
trees that grow.
We open the window and
all we see is
life appearing to us,
but we are part of
life's big circle
that comes and goes.

Lucy Waldron (14)
William Bradford Community College

THEM!

It's so easy for the teachers,
they think they understand,
'Just ignore them,' they say,
but they just won't go away.

They say they're still my friends,
that's what makes it worse,
when they won't say a civil word
to my other friend. That hurts!

They still talk to me occasionally,
it really makes me sad
to think that they can be so nice,
when usually they're bad.

They write us nasty letters,
calling her names,
it's only one they bully
but it affects us all the same!

Helen Porter (14)
William Bradford Community College

AUTUMN

A bed of acorns and conkers litters the floor.
A multitude of colours fills the sky,
As the royal gold leaves flutter mindlessly to the ground.
Animals scurrying back and forth
As the birds soar high in the sky
And the scrunch of the leaves as you walk
Along the frosty pathway.

Autumn is here!

Phillip Sparks (14)
William Bradford Community College

SEVEN-NIL

Kick! and the match starts with a flourish,
first-aiders sidelined ready to nourish.
We, Barwell FC, conjure up our first bit of pressure,
But comes to no effect at a certain measure.
The other team swaggered round the field,
Our weaknesses you might say were revealed.
They had this really pacey striker and his name I think was Ben,
Our side just never knew what hit them.

Our coach (beetroot red) yelled insults and abuse,
Even his tactics didn't seem much use.
Their tackles and goals seemed mean and cruel,
Nobody on our side was looking cool.
Full time approached and I began to think of just what to say,
As our team limped off at the close of play.
They were just too good I began to announce,
In front of my team, rudely trounced.

In the car home not a word was said,
I just thought of drowning the sorrow in a nice, warm bed.

Sam Allen (14)
William Bradford Community College

BEING ME

It's not about listening to heavy metal,
And it's not about dying your hair green.

It's not about trying to scare people,
And it's not about trying different extreme sports.

One thing that it is about . . .
Is being me.

Nathan Sands (14)
William Bradford Community College

EURO 2000 'THE DREAM'

Shearer leads out his talented England team,
Would Euro 2000 be a nightmare or dream?
As England line up with hearts in their mouths,
They proudly sing the National Anthem aloud.
England kick off to the stadium's mighty roar,
All the fans hoping for the very best score.
Owen pulls back his trusty right foot and lets one fly,
When the ball hits the net the keeper wishes he could
Curl up and die.
As England's goals flood in one by one,
The opposing team's score is still at none.
England's fans are all doing the 'wave'
The other half just sits there in a daze.
As full time approaches and the cup almost won,
Keegan sits back, it's a job well done.
The trophy is lifted and the players are happy,
Beckham goes home to change Brooklyn's nappy.

Justin Heath (14)
William Bradford Community College

MEMORIES

Nineteen years is quite a while
Since you walked up the aisle.

On a slightly warm September's day
You couldn't tell Dad's hair was grey.

I bet you've had such a blast
Reminiscing about the past.

You've always been so very great,
The parents you just love to hate.

Claire Wassell (14)
William Bradford Community College

THE ICE DESERT

As you wander through this place,
All around is white,
Your fingers start to tingle,
And you feel no delight.

You start to wonder why,
You do not see the point,
You feel all alone,
On a wide extensive site.

As you delve into the mist,
You see a twinkle of light,
You continue up the gully,
You see no glimmer of this mysterious sight.

You might as well turn back,
But when that moment hits you,
You feel above the rest,
Sitting on a bed of mist, you're high above the rest.

Andrew Gregson (14)
William Bradford Community College

A WINTER'S MORNING

Waking up to a cold, frosty morning,
Open the door and breathe in the cold, crisp air.
The sun shines down brightly,
Reflecting the silver drops of ice water.
Brighter the sun shines, till no trace
Of that perfect, cold, crisp morning
Is any more.

Rebecca Lewis (14)
William Bradford Community College

UNDERSTAND

He is standing unaware
Of what he may not know.
He stares into space,
Gloomy eyed, but
Not fascinated in the passers-by.

He stands with ears laid back,
For what reasons we'll never know.
He is thin and his ribs are present,
With teeth bared,
He is so scared.

His eyes are dark,
And his soul is too.
His heart is empty,
No love.
No hope.

He circles around and around
For what seems like forever.
One nod and he is gone,
To a man,
A slaughter man.

He was not the only one there,
Thousands more are unaware
Of their fate.
Maybe life, maybe death,
It depends on who is there.

Michelle Stretton (14)
William Bradford Community College

MY GRANDMA

My grandma lives in a bungalow,
The stairs are painted green,
The garden's as small as a postage stamp,
The largest I've ever seen.

You can't see through the windows,
And what a lovely view,
Nothing's ever finished
And there's nothing left to do.

Next morning at 6 pm
She has breakfast for her tea,
Her locked doors are always open
And everything she buys is free.

If it's fixed, it's always broken,
If it's broken there's nothing wrong,
The lounge is wide and narrow,
The landing's short and long.

She hasn't got a telly,
But watches 'Good Morning' every night,
She has a paper every evening
Delivered at first light.

My grandma's house is paradise,
I've hated going there,
The best place ever in the world,
But it isn't there.

Paul Coleman (14)
William Bradford Community College

SUB

Sub again! It makes me sick.
It wouldn't matter if we ever won,
But we're losing, no surprise.
Last Tuesday night, we lost 6-1.

Why don't I ever get picked?
I've done nothing wrong.
Hey, what's the manager saying now,
'Go on for Charles who's hurt his knee.'
This should be more fun.

I'm on, I get a kick,
I pass to Carl who passes to John.
John accelerates down the wing,
An opposition tries to tackle but John is too fast.
He kicks the ball, it's coming towards me,
I chest it down and I can see
That the keeper is coming towards me.
Now it's just one on one,
I get past the keeper. Yes! I score.
1-1.

Mark Statham (14)
William Bradford Community College

CANDLE

Glowing so bright,
flickering like light,
keeping the place so alight
all the way through the night.

Glowing so bright
like the stars at night,
reminds me of
the moon that night.

As the day dawns
the flame that reigns
keeps flickering on
until another day dawns.

Vicky Keen (14)
William Bradford Community College

I AM...

I am the sunlight of every great day,
I am the wind that blows you away,
I am that place where we'd all love to stay.

I am the night who plays tricks on your mind,
I am the friend who'd never leave you behind,
I am that treasure we all hope to find.

I am your dreams that live in the sky,
I am that scene pleasing to your eyes.

I am the universe, vast and untamed,
I am that feeling you just can't explain.

I am that love who'd stay true to my dear,
I am that wish which is secret in you,
I am that time which we'd all love to have,
I am everything you'd ever love to own,
I am the spirit that hides deep in you,
I am that keepsake you couldn't live without.

I am everything good that could happen in life,
I am whatever you want me to be - something different
for everybody.

Victoria Ward (14)
William Bradford Community College

FEELING

The heat burns through my body,
Tossed and turned by an ocean of grief,
A dagger in my heart.
A pain so deep it tears through my soul,
I care not for life,
I have been cheated.
An angry world eats away at my guilt-ridden body.
The scars of eternal hatred,
Crushed.
Twisting, turning, fighting,
There's no way out.
Trapped, tied down by the chains of life,
Tormented by my thoughts,
A fiery, bloodstained fate.

Sophie Moore (15)
William Bradford Community College

NIGHT

It comes devouring everything in its path,
Causing darkness and despair where it goes,
Like a black knight on a dark steed.

Then comes the holy light,
It chases away the dark,
Only to come the next night,
Twice as strong.

Ever bigger, stronger,
Spreading its thickness
Over the land.

Kieron Leeson (14)
William Bradford Community College

My Hope For The Future

My hope for the future is to be a vet,
I might be able to adopt a pet,
A cat, a dog or a budgerigar,
My concern is that its life will go far.

My hope for the future is not to get married,
Not even a baby by me will be carried,
Babies are smelly, they wake you by crying,
Husband's bad habits I am not buying.

My hope for the future is to be cremated,
Being buried in a coffin I have always hated,
I want to be visited every week,
Right until my visitors have reached their peak!

Reanne Leatherland (14)
William Bradford Community College

Future Voices

F   lying saucers everywhere,
U   nusual, frightening, I was scared,
T   ortured minds,
U   nknown things,
R   un quick,
E   nemies invading,

V   oices screaming,
O   ver there,
I   n their homes,
C   rying children
E   verywhere,
S   creaming!

Kerry Chamberlain (14)
William Bradford Community College

THE NUMBING

Sweetness is a virtue,
I've been waiting just to kill you,
But my conscience tells me no,
No emotion I should show.

When you took everything from me,
I was blind to see
I never wanted to die,
I just wanted an excuse to cry.
I need everything from tomorrow,
Just to defeat my innermost sorrow,
With all the people talking,
It's driving me mad
With such a happy face,
Why do I feel so sad.

Something has died,
Maybe I should start to hide.
I wanna laugh myself to death.
I'll hold the line while you gasp for breath.

My distorted smile,
It will make you run a mile.
Have some fun with my frustration.
Through your sadness
I'll find salvation.

Vicki Allen (14)
William Bradford Community College

THE BOY = GUILT

We went on a trip down to London one day,
My mum and I and some others,
And we saw a boy about fifteen or more,
Over him were some old, tattered covers.

We wanted to stop but the others walked on,
And we didn't know our way to the bus,
We stood there and watched as he shivered with cold,
And saw he was staring at us.

He stretched out his hand,
A woman shouted the bus was ready to leave,
As we turned away and walked around the corner,
His face was like nothing I could believe.

On the way home I looked out from the bus,
The sky was a delightful deep red,
I forgot about the boy on the roadside,
And the fact he'd probably be dead.

But from that day on,
I still feel the guilt
About the boy on the roadside,
With that tattered, old quilt.

Lee Fulton (14)
William Bradford Community College

WILL IT BE?

Will it be big? Will it be small?
Will Earth exist at all?
Will it be black or will it be white?
All the answers end in might.

Will aliens be more than UFOs,
Or will it be the same, who knows?
Will we walk on ground or air?
All these questions we all share.

Will Earth be a haven or maybe a hell,
How can we be certain,
How can we tell?

One thing's for sure and there is no doubt.
There's always more to know
And find out!

Samantha Abbott (14)
William Bradford Community College

A WINTER'S MORN

It was a cold, crisp winter's morn,
The birds sang their morning song,
Hopping about to keep themselves warm.

Sharp icicles hung from overhangs as steep as cliffs,
Like assassin's blades poised above victims.

Frost glazed over windows making them as
Sheets of vertical sea,
Jack Frost had been at work.

Thomas Vavasour (15)
William Bradford Community College

FUTURE VOICES

In twenty years or more,
will there be peace or
will there be war?
Will there be children playing around?
Will everybody be safe and sound?

I hope they get rid of all that sadness,
'Cause deep down inside they will find gladness,
I hope they will be satisfied with what they have got,
because some people will have it, others might not.

All I can think is what the future may bring,
but there is just one little thing,
I want the future to be happy and bright
and for no one to ever fight.
I admit the future will not be great,
but make the most of it before it's too late.

Michelle Ashby (14)
William Bradford Community College

CHOCOLATE

Chocolate in my dreams,
Heavenly smell,
Only one day without chocolate, I would melt away,
Coco Pops first thing in the morning,
Oh what would it be like to swim in it?
Lovely and smooth, you could float away,
A favourite chocolate of mine, white-centred Aero,
Terror nightmare, having no chocolate,
Eating it all day would be a dream in heaven.

Jenna Liney (14)
William Bradford Community College

FUTURE VOICES

When I grow up I'll listen to my dad
Go to work and earn a wage,
Cough up some rent because of my age,
Get a nice little car,
Drive to villages not too far.

When I grow up I won't listen to Blair,
Maggie Thatcher, none of them, it's just not fair.
Get a secure job and go somewhere in life.

When I grow up I'll listen to my friends,
Hear what they have to say.
Something good, it all depends.

When I grow up I'll listen to the people
Around me. Stick by my friends,
Support each other, you know the score.

Go somewhere in life, settle down,
Begin a family and have a gorgeous wife.

Tom Coleburne (15)
William Bradford Community College

PARENTS

Parents can be a bit of a pain,
Sometimes they can even drive you insane.
If they weren't around,
We'd all be in vain.

They hug us and bug us,
Ground us, then we're sad,
Then we're very, very bad.

Aimee Gibbs (14)
William Bradford Community College

LIFE'S POSSIBILITIES

Maybe I will be a football superstar,
Will I end up in a ruck or maul?
Will I play in a cricket cathedral, the new Hobbs or even Hadlee?
Maybe I will hit the winning Wimbledon ace.

Maybe I will end up a drunken yob,
Or maybe I will be another crime statistic.
Will I end up in social care,
Will I be one of life's failures?

Maybe I will be the next Arthur Lowe or John Le Messurier.
Will I be the next Phil Collins or even Slow Hand,
Will I end up an excellent entrepreneur?
Maybe I will be a billionaire, living the high life in Bridgetown.

The future is still to be written.
Our actions and behaviour shape what we are!

Scott Burns (14)
William Bradford Community College

WINTER

Frost on the window,
snow on the floor,
icicles hanging
and cold feet sore.
People on sledges,
having a laugh,
parents at home feeling a draught.
Logs on the fire,
hot food nearby,
waiting for children to come in from
outside . . .

Wayne Klenk (14)
William Bradford Community College

LIFE'S LIFE

Everything changes, nothing's the same,
One day we're here, the next there,
Down life's endless lane.

People change, they will move on,
One day we're there, the next we're gone.
Nobody knows how long they've got,
When time's up, it's up.
There's no clock.

Live life to the max, never relax,
Live for the moment, don't be dormant.
Be there to erupt, have your own fun.

You think you'll be around forever,
But never forever.
Everything will change.
Don't mope or give up hope,
Change with life,
After all, you don't know what you've got . . .
'Til it's gone.

Paul Boddington (14)
William Bradford Community College

ALIENS

Aliens here, aliens there,
Where to run? Over there.
We run fast, don't know where,
We ran every where.
We saw a sign, said 'Beware,
Aliens landing over there.'

Sam Strain (14)
William Bradford Community College

THE OBSESSIVE CRUSH

When I was eight years old,
I had a new crush.
There was a new boy band around,
All five members were in their teens,
Not one had a ring on the left hand.

Now the boy I like is short but sweet,
He's the one I'd love to meet.
He has black hair and gazing blue eyes,
When I see him my heart just dies.
When I hear him on the radio I have tears in my eyes,
He looks so good I could eat him up . . .
Or drink him out of a cup.

When I was thirteen there was terrible news,
The boy announced he had bad news,
He said he was gay,
I still love this boy today . . .
Although he's gone away.

Now I'll say that this boy is absolutely gorgeous
And that's my new Obsessive Crush.

Lynn Ison (14)
William Bradford Community College

CHOCOLATE FUDGE CAKE

Chocolate fudge cake is so yummy,
It feels so good when it's in your tummy.
It tastes really good with all that fudge,
If anyone touches it I'll give them a nudge.

Claire Burrows (14)
William Bradford Community College

WONDERFUL THOUGHTS

How wonderful it would be
to lay on a bed of green, lush grass
and look above contentedly.
I would lie alone and look into the sky
and watch the clouds as they
passed gently by.
How relaxing it could be, no noise,
no fuss - only me.
I'd concentrate hard on the shapes above,
a lion, a tiger, a soaring white dove,
I'd see how many figures I could make out,
then close my eyes and let them jump out.
Bye, bye for now, nice thoughts, I'll put you to bed
and next time I'm down here again,
I'll look at the clouds,
so more figures can enter my head.

Kate Welland (14)
William Bradford Community College

LIFE

Life is like a football team,
Your first kick of a ball, now you're born,
Now you know the basics, now you're at school,
Now you've made the team,
Now you're on your way in life,
Trying to keep your position,
The pain of the teenage years,
In a professional team, at the peak of life, manhood,
Struggling with injuries, old age is near,
Now you're retired. Guess what comes next?

Gareth Granger (15)
William Bradford Community College

MATCH SUSPENCE

Scampering out of what they call a tunnel
To the crowds' explosive roar,
A family of team mates eager to perform,
They line up in order,
Defence,
Midfield,
Attack.

The kits all gleaming, freshly washed,
It starts, running round frantically to get the ball,
To show the national coach what he's missing.
The game goes backwards and forwards,
Takes dramatic turns,
The stadium seems like a night of thunder and lightning,
Them calling your name more and more.

It comes to a close, everyone leaves the pitch,
But we're still sulking on the ground.
We lost the FA Cup Final.

Ryan Measham (14)
William Bradford Community College

I HAVE NOT

I have not run through a meadow of burning hot coals,
I have not killed,
Or even stolen,
I have not fought battles in distant countries,
I have not made life-threatening decisions,
But at the end of the day
At least I can say,
I have lived.

Shaun Smith (14)
William Bradford Community College

COLD, FROSTY MORNING

The frosty ground shone brightly all around,
With cobwebs hanging high all around.
Spiders huddle tightly in their webs,
While flies pass by avoiding the webs.

Humans below, all cuddled and warmed,
While the tiny creatures struggle for warmth.
Hats and gloves are perfect for us,
While fur and feathers are not as good.

With cloudy skies way above,
Why should we be dull when we have frost.
Mr Jack Frost put a spell on me,
As I wait to be as sparkly as you.

Victoria Borley (14)
William Bradford Community College

DINOSAUR

Imagine a dinosaur, big and angry,
Imagine a dinosaur with teeth as sharp
                  as razor blades,
Imagine a dinosaur with skin as rough
                  as sand paper,
Imagine a dinosaur, different colours from
Dark green to bright purple, with yellow spots.
Imagine a dinosaur as big as a house,
Imagine a human as small as a little, green pea.
If you see a dinosaur, you turn and run,
But if it catches you, you don't stand a chance.

Shaun Masterman (14)
William Bradford Community College

WAR ZONE

A great silence falls over the land,
Simple but lethal explosions have shattered our lives.
Our world destroyed in an instant,
By mindless soldiers following orders from above.
As the thick, black smog entered our hearts,
We prayed.

The ill and wounded lay paralysed and in pain.
Sticks of dynamite containing nitro-glycerine
Continued to kill the innocent.
Thousands dead,
Even more injured.

I guess this is what they call a 'War Zone.'

Sam Woodhouse (14)
William Bradford Community College

CHEETAH

Sliding smoothly through the undergrowth,
ready to pounce on an unsuspecting creature,
springing into action at the sight of a lone,
vulnerable antelope,
its slimline body portraying the brute strength behind
its powerful shoulders.

Roaming the vast plains of Africa,
marking its territory, finding freedom on the open savannah,
demanding the respect of other animals,
this yellowish-brown spotted cat is the fastest land-living
creature that exists.

Clare Moore (15)
William Bradford Community College

FUTURE HOPES

My hopes for the future
are to be a millionaire.

Have lots of money
and never have a care.

Look after the ill
and give to the poor.

To have a big car,
to own lots of stores.

Have loads of houses all around the world,
for people to stay in when they're abroad.

My hopes for the future seem so far away,
so I will be working hard every day.

Rebecca Tallis (14)
William Bradford Community College

FUTURE VOICE

Maybe in the future our children
Will not be free, but
Slaves to the alien impostors.

The short, green men will kill
Our planet Earth before moving
Onto the next planet.

The survivors of these abominations
Will die of starvation or disease
And the Earth will return to peace.

Laura Adcock (14)
William Bradford Community College

ANIMALS

A budgie lives in a cage,
Lions roar with rage,
The trees, the breeze,
The monkeys swinging in the trees,
The giraffe has a really long neck,
While at the tree,
The woodpecker pecks,
The cats and dogs
Walking in the street,
Miaowing, woofing as they meet.
The monkeys chatter,
The fish turn to batter,
The rabbits sit eating carrots.
Amongst all the squawking parrots,
There's a zebra black and white,
Walking cautiously in the night.

Hayley Roper (14)
William Bradford Community College

DREAMING

I love to drift to this far off place,
feeling warm and that tingly feeling
of the sun on my face.

The feeling of floating along in peace,
that feeling of relaxed tranquillity -
that moment I want to cease.

No worries, no blunders,
this land is full of the wonders
of dreaming.

Leah Benness (14)
William Bradford Community College

FUTURE VOICES

The future world is full of pollution,
So now it's time for children's revolution.
A clean, fresh world is what we need,
So we must stand up for what we believe.

This is our planet, not by choice,
We speak together as one voice.
This air we breathe, don't take it for granted,
Don't let the seeds of doom be planted.

In every nation on the Earth,
Let my message be given birth.
Let's not just take, but also give,
As this is where we have to live.

Samantha Chamberlain (14)
William Bradford Community College

UNEXPECTED

It was the 'unexpectancy' which shocked people.
No one actually thought it could or would happen,
But it did
And everyone hid.

Aliens! People would scream,
Hoping it was all just a dream.
Where would they run?
Where would they hide?
People needed someone in whom they could confide.

But it wasn't as scary as they made out.
The aliens just wanted to help out.

Laura Skelham (14)
William Bradford Community College

WHY DID THEY CHOOSE ME?

I've never painted a perfect picture,
Or written a winning poem,
I've never been good at games,
Or been chosen for the cross-country team,
I've never been outstanding in any of my lessons,
Or had brilliant exam marks.

Why did they choose me?
Have they made a big mistake?
Do they think they have picked
The shiniest gem
From the centre of a tray?
So why did they choose me?

Anneka Bradley (14)
William Bradford Community College

THE CAVE

I was walking through the big, dark green forest,
When I saw the big, dark black hole,
The cave,
So I walked closer.
All I could hear was the drip, drip dripping
Of the wet mossy walls.
The smell of rot was almost unbearable,
But I went in anyway,
And that's when I saw it.
The big, scary creature with all the legs,
The spider.
So I ran.

Helen McShane (14)
William Bradford Community College

WHAT WILL WE BE?

We are told 'The future is bright.'
Robots will fulfil our insatiable demand,
Microchips will abolish crime and
Lessons will happen in a flash.

But,

Will we have any privacy?
Will there be such a thing as fun?
Will we be told off for not eating our greens?
Will we have a job from eight to ninety-eight?

Will the 'future' be mankind's downfall?

Tim Casalis de Pury (14)
William Bradford Community College

FUTURE VOICES

If I'm honest, I am afraid to get older,
I'm afraid to watch the world change.
I'm afraid to lose the people I love.
Life,
Life can be a fantastic dream
That you never want to leave,
Or it can be a dreadful nightmare
That you can't wait to get out of,
But unlike dreams, life carries on,
Even if you are afraid.

Melanie Horak (14)
William Bradford Community College

FUTURE VOICES

As life goes on,
People move on.

The saddest time for me
Is when family has gone.

Friends are a part of my life,
They help as I struggle through my strife.

In the past, future
Voices have called me forward.

For future, ambitions, but
Those ambitions have eventually faded.

There is a corner of my life which is shaded,
A future job.

I realise as I grow
I will need to work to live

And that everything I have, cannot
Just be someone else's handout.

As life beckons before me,
I teach myself all I need to know about

Myself and my own personality,
And my expectations of my

Single life.

Hayley Shaw (14)
William Bradford Community College

LIGHTLESS LIGHT

The sun rises,
But darkness remains,
Birds sing,
Meaningless groans,
Emptiness.

> The wind blows
> Yet all remains still,
> Young children playing together,
> An exercise drill,
> Emptiness.

> > A babbling brook - silent,
> > A noiseless clap of thunder,
> > A grey tulip,
> > Emptiness.

> Looking down from unbreaking night
> Perched on a cloud, eyes still bright,
> Your chance at life came and went,
> Thinking what it really meant.

You have gone,
Far away,
Leaving me,
A heart of clay.

Julian Sayarer (14)
William Bradford Community College

ALIENS

It came down the silver stairs,
Not bothered by the looks, glances, stares.
The world held its breath
As the visitors came from right and left.

No one could ever understand
From exactly which land
These creatures were made,
But their first words were 'Don't be afraid.'

Richard Chamberlain (14)
William Bradford Community College

SILENCE IN THE LAND

The bombs they come,
Silently, stealthily,
Exploding into vivid, colourful clouds.
Creeping like cautious fingers of death,
Radiation seeps into the soil,
Fear embraces the land.

People vaporised, no longer breathing,
Lie silent and singed.
Majestic buildings no longer stand tall and proud,
They squat dismally, a jumbled rubble of stone,
Desolation in the land.

The molten sky rains warheads,
Cascading black rain onto corpses and the living remains,
Facing slow, torturous deaths.
Fear tainting their memories forever.
Poisoned - the land.

The devastated landscape no longer thrives,
Survivors roam like haunted souls,
Searching for lost loved ones never to be found.
Is there no hope for them?
Silence in the land.

Kirsty Smith (14)
William Bradford Community College

YELLOW IS . . .

Yellow is the colour of the sunshine bright,
Yellow is the colour of the moon at night,
Yellow is the colour that I think's brill,
Yellow is the colour of the dancing daffodil,
Yellow is the colour that reminds me of spring,
Yellow is the colour that makes me want to sing,
Yellow is the colour of day not night,
Yellow is the colour that I think's bright!

Gemma Sharman (14)
William Bradford Community College

HAVE YOU EVER?

Have you ever thought about what the future will be like?
Calm, exotic, safe!
Or will it stay the way it is now,
Dull, ugly, dangerous?
Have you ever thought of what the people may be like?
Friendly and fun! Nasty and deadly!
Have you ever considered the future at all?

Rowena Feary (14)
William Bradford Community College

SPORT

Sport is something that I like,
Whether it be on my feet or on my bike.
Watersports attract my attention,
Far too many for me to mention.
Athletics is the thing I like best,
Even though I enjoy all the rest.

Zoe Thompson (14)
William Bradford Community College

2000 VOICES

Have you ever closed your eyes
And listened to the people around you
That you know and love?

There's Grandma, interfering with the Christmas cake,
And Grandpa playing with the dog.
Then your brother and his girlfriend trying to get a quick snog,
Before Mum comes in with party-poppers singing
Jingle Bells.
What with Aunty Flo moaning that the baby smells,
Uncle Bob sits there flirting with Aunty Flo,
Whips the baby out of her arms and tells your Dad,
'Two sherries to go.'
Next in comes your younger sister with all her new toys,
We all sit around watching her until Grandpa
Wants to play with a Polly Dolly too.

These annual family gatherings that you know
Won't last forever,
But really when you tell them to shut up for just two minutes,
You really want to freeze time and make the moment last eternally,
So that none of the 2000 voices around you
Ever fade away and disappear forever.

Even though you know that some day in the future,
You won't be watching Grandpa fall asleep in his wobbly old chair,
Any more.

Michelle Percival (14)
William Bradford Community College

FUTURE VOICES

I live in outer space,
Along with the other members of my intergalactic race.
Our planet is a wondrous sight,
With spiralling colours throughout the night.

Whizzing around are flying cars,
Which originated back on Mars.
Their bodies glow with gold and steel
And special metal that we call 'phliel.'

Giant ships gather in space
For a competition known as 'The Chase.'
Each one tries to get in the lead,
Travelling as fast as light speed.

Tablet meals are all we take,
Unlike in history when they had steak.
How strange were people in the past,
It's amazing how they were able to last.

We all live in a large dome,
With giant tunnels in which we roam.
Our rooms are large and full of space,
It is truly a beautiful, tranquil place.

Outer space is the place to be,
So many wondrous things to see.
The beings are so kind and good,
Visit us now, you know you should.

Katie Potter (14)
William Bradford Community College

FUTURE VOICES

Help!
Help!
Please someone help.

Where is the voice coming from?
The future!
The future!

The sky is dark and smoky,
The air is acrid and burns my
Throat when I gulp for air.

The flowers are long and distant memories.
The bees have nowhere to go.

What is the matter O future voice?
Man is the matter my child.
He has polluted the Earth, the sky and
The future with toxic greed.

You are the future, it is up to you
To alter the scheme of things.

Plant flowers my child, not seeds of doubt.
Save the planet for your future voices.

Life is in your hands now!

Rebecca Payne (14)
William Bradford Community College

NEXT GENERATION

First came the Nes,
and then came the Snes,
technology back then
could be explained as a den,
it's cold, dark and mysterious.

Later on came the Megadrive,
which frightfully took a dive.
To take advantage of Sega's defeat,
Nintendo brought out the Game Boy.

The 'Boy' reigned long,
but not for long,
because Sony had a plan.

They gave the PlayStation 1 & 2
to a different crowd,
which saw their money fly,
but then came out a different one, loud one.

Nintendo 64, oh 'ninety' have scored,
but lagging behind is Sega's Dreamcast,
O, what a bore.

And finally, came the Nintendo Dolphin.
What will the world bring next?

Ian Stock (14)
William Bradford Community College

WHAT COLOUR IS THE WORLD

The world is blue,
with sky and sea,
with people like you and me,
the world is danger, full of adventure.

The world is yellow
with the shining sun,
which brings day and light
into the night.

The world is green
with grazing grass,
with sheep and cows
which never pass.

The world is orange
with sunrise and sunset,
we are filled with surprise
as well as delight.

The world is purple,
full of power and might,
we are ruled by people who have to fight.

The world is good,
the world is bad,
but which and what
colour is the world!

Amy Webb (14)
William Bradford Community College

THAT MOMENT WHEN

That moment when
You first see him,
Across the school hall.
His thick, shiny hair,
His beautiful blue eyes,
You're standing there
Unaware,
You're in a stare.

That moment when
You make a new friend,
Someone to laugh with,
Talk with and cry with,
The person who'll listen,
The person who'll comfort,
The person who'll be there,
The person who'll care.

That moment when
A loved one dies,
The emptiness inside,
And the months of mourning,
The endless sound of crying,
people wearing black,
At that point in time,
You know they're not coming back.

That moment when.

Hannah Botterill (14)
William Bradford Community College